PHILOSOPHY IN TURBULENT TIMES

Elisabeth ROUDINESCO

TRANSLATED BY William McCUAIG

PHILOSOPHY IN TURBULENT TIMES
CANGUILHEM, SARTRE

COLUMBIA UNIVERSITY PRESS *New York*

FOUCAULT, ALTHUSSER, DELEUZE, DERRIDA

Columbia University Press
Publishers Since 1893
New York   Chichester, West Sussex

Library of Congress Cataloging-in-Publication
Roudinesco, Elisabeth, 1944–
[Philosophes dans la tourmente. English]
Philosophy in turbulent times: Canguilhem,
Sartre, Foucault, Althusser, Deleuze,
Derrida / Elisabeth Roudinesco; translated by
William McCuaig.
p. cm.
Includes bibliographical references (p.   ).
ISBN 978-0-231-14300-4 (cloth: alk.
paper)—ISBN 978-0-231-51885-7 (e-book)
1. Philosophy—France—History—20th
century. 2. Philosophy, French—20th
century. 3. Philosophers—France—History—
20th century. I. Title.
B2421.R6813   2008
194—dc22
2008021953

Columbia University Press books are printed on
permanent and durable acid-free paper.

Printed in the United States of America
c 10 9 8 7 6 5 4 3 2 1

To Christian Jambet

CONTENTS

INTRODUCTION

{In Defense of Critical Thought}

W E ARE CERTAINLY LIVING IN STRANGE TIMES. The commemoration of great events, great men, great intellectual achievements, and great virtues never stops; we've had the year of Rimbaud, the year of Victor Hugo, the year of Jules Verne. And yet, never have revisionist attacks on the foundations of every discipline, every doctrine, every emancipatory adventure enjoyed such prestige. Feminism, socialism, and psychoanalysis are violently rejected, and Freud, Marx, and Nietzsche are pronounced dead, along with every kind of critique of the norm. All we are entitled to do, it would seem, is to take stock and draw up assessments, as though the distance that every intellectual enterprise requires amounted to no more than a vast ledger full of entries for things and people—or rather people who have become things.

I am not thinking just of Holocaust denial, which has been outlawed among professional historians, although its influence persists in semisecrecy. Instead what I have in mind are those ordinary little revisionisms that tend, for example, to put Vichy and the Resistance on the same footing, because of the "necessity" to relativize heroism, and the drive to oppugn the idea of rebellion. Another example is the clever reinterpretation of textual evidence to make Salvador Allende into a racist, an anti-Semite, and a eugenicist, for the purpose of denigrating the putative founding myths of socialism around the world.[1]

As for philosophy, while its place in the educational curriculum of the schools and universities is threatened by all those who judge it useless, outmoded, too Greek or too German, and impossible to put a price on or fit into a scientistic pigeonhole (in sum, too subversive), the drive to "philosophize" or "learn to think for oneself" is expanding outside the institutions of the state, embracing Plato, Socrates, the pre-Socratic materialists, the Latins, the moderns, the postmoderns, the old and new moderns, the new or old reactionaries. There is a gap between the academicism that is returning in force to official schooling and the massive demand for "living" teaching outside the universities, and this gap continues to grow wider in a world haunted by fear of the loss of identity, boundaries, and national particularism.

Feature stories in our periodicals and newspapers almost all convey a catastrophic outlook: the end of history, the end of ideology, the end of towering individuals, the end of thought, the end of mankind, the end of everything. Jean-Paul Sartre—for or against? Raymond Aron—for or against? Would it suit you better to be in the right with the former as against the latter, or vice versa? Should we take a blowtorch to May 1968 and its ideas, its thinkers, and their writings, seen now as incomprehensible, elitist, dangerous, and antidemocratic? Have the protagonists of that revolution in behavior and mentality all become little bourgeois capitalist pleasure seekers without faith or principles, or haven't they?

Everywhere the same questions, and everywhere the same answers, all claiming to bear witness to a new malaise of civilization. The father has vanished, but why not the mother? Isn't the mother really just a father, in the end, and the father a mother? Why do young people not think anything? Why are children so unbearable? Is it because of Françoise Dolto, or television, or pornography, or comic books? And leading thinkers—what has become of them? Are they dead, or gestating, or hibernating? Or are they on the road to extinction?

And women: are they capable of supervising male workers on the same basis as men are? Of thinking like men, of being philosophers? Do they have the same brain, the same neurons, the same emotions, the same criminal instincts? Was Christ the lover of Mary Magdalene, and if so, does that mean that the Christian religion is sexually split between a hidden feminine pole and a dominant masculine one?

Has France become decadent? Are you for Spinoza, Darwin, Galileo, or against? Are you partial to the United States? Wasn't Heidegger a Nazi? Was Michel Foucault the precursor of Bin Laden, Gilles Deleuze a drug addict, Jacques Derrida a deconstructed guru? Was Napoleon really so different from Hitler? State the similarities, proffer your thoughts, assess your knowledge, speak for yourself.

Whom do you prefer; who are the puniest figures, the greatest ones, the most mediocre, the biggest charlatans, the most criminal? Classify, rank, calculate, measure, put a price on, normalize: this is the absolute nadir of contemporary interrogation, endlessly imposing itself in the name of a bogus modernity that undermines every form of critical intelligence grounded in the analysis of the complexity of things and persons.

Never has sexuality been so untrammeled, and never has science progressed so far in the exploration of the body and the brain. Yet never has psychological suffering been more intense: solitude, use of mind-altering drugs, boredom, fatigue, dieting, obesity, the medicalization of every second of existence. The freedom of the self, so necessary, and won at the cost of so much struggle during the twentieth century, seems to have turned back into a demand for puritanical restraint. As for social suffering, it is increasingly harder to bear because it seems to be constantly on the rise, against a background of youth unemployment and tragic factory closings.

Set free from the shackles of morality, sex is experienced not as the correlate of desire, but as performance, as gymnastics, as hygiene for the organs that can only lead to deathly lassitude. How does one climax, and bring one's partner to climax. What is the ideal size of the vagina, the correct length of the penis? How often? How many partners in a lifetime, in a week, in a single day, minute by minute? Never has the psychology of conditioning, of sexological or partner-swapping alienation been so overpowering as it is today. So much so that by now we are seeing a surge in complaints of every kind. The more individuals are promised happiness and the ideal of security, the more their unhappiness persists, the steeper the risk profile grows, and the more the victims of unkept promises revolt against those who have betrayed them.

It would seem impossible not to detect, in this curious psychologization of existence that has gripped society and that is contributing to the rise of depoliticization, the most insidious expression of what Michel Foucault and Gilles Deleuze called "little everyday fascism," intimate, desired, longed-for, admitted, and celebrated by the very individual who is both its protagonist and its victim. A little fascism, which of course has nothing to do with the great fascist systems, since it slips inside each individual without his realizing it, without ever calling into question the sacrosanct principles of the rights of man, of humanism, of democracy.

I have chosen to render homage to six French philosophers—Canguilhem, Sartre, Foucault, Althusser, Deleuze, and Derrida—whose work is known and discussed throughout the world, and who, despite their divergences, their disputes, and the impulses they shared, had this in common: they all confronted, in a critical fashion, not just the question of political engagement (meaning a philosophy of freedom) but also the Freudian concept of the unconscious (meaning a philosophy of structure). They all commanded a literary style, and they were all passionate about art and literature.

This confrontation was inscribed in their works and their lives, and that is why it is fitting to bring them together here. They all refused, at the price of what I would call a passage through the tempest, to serve the project to normalize the human being—a project that, in its most experimental version, is no more than an ideology of submission in the service of barbarity. Each of them published his oeuvre in an age before television and other media had the importance they now have in the transmission of knowledge, and two of them, Deleuze and Derrida, laid the basis for new ways of thinking about the logic of the modern media.

Far from commemorating their former glory or devoting myself nostalgically to a simple recapitulation of their works, I have tried, by making the thought of some operate through the thought of others, and by highlighting some of the leading moments of the history of French intellectual life in the second half of the twentieth century, to show that only the critical acceptance of a heritage makes it possible to think for oneself and to invent the thought of the future, a thought for better times, a thought that refuses to submit, a thought unfaithful out of necessity.

NOTES ON THE TEXT

S OME CHAPTERS OF THIS BOOK ARE DERIVED FROM TEXTS
published in different form.

An early version of chapter 1, "Georges Canguilhem: A Philosophy
of Heroism," was presented at the tenth colloquy of the Société internationale d'histoire de la psychiatrie et de la psychanalyse (International
Society for the History of Psychiatry and Psychoanalysis), held in Paris
in December 1993. The colloquy was dedicated to the fiftieth anniversary of the publication of Georges Canguilhem's thesis, *Le normal et le
pathologique*. The conference papers were published in 1998 as *Actualités
de Georges Canguilhem* (Paris: Institut Synthélabo), with contributions
by François Bing, Jean-François Braunstein, Rene Major, Georges Lan-
téri-Laura, Henri Péquignot, Pierre Macherey, and François Dagog-
net, and an interview with Georges Canguilhem. See as well Élisabeth
Roudinesco, "Situation d'un texte: 'Qu'est-ce que la psychologie?'" in
Georges Canguilhem: Philosophe, historien des sciences (Paris: Albin Michel, 1993 [in the series Bibliothèque du collège international de philoso-
phie], 135–44).

A shorter version of chapter 2, "Jean-Paul Sartre: Psychoanalysis on the Shadowy Banks of the Danube," was published as "Sartre, lecteur de Freud," in *Les Temps Modernes* nos. 531–33 (December 1990): 590–613.

Chapter 3, "Michel Foucault: Readings of *History of Madness*," appeared in different form in *Penser la folie: Essais sur Michel Foucault* (Paris: Galilée, 1992). The other contributors were Georges Canguilhem, Jacques Postel, François Bing, Arlette Farge, Claude Quétel, Agostino Pirellea, René Major, and Jacques Derrida.

Chapter 6, "Jacques Derrida: The Moment of Death," was first published as "—Athos, Porthos, au revoir—Aramis, à jamais, adieu!" in *Cahiers de l'Herne* 83 (2004), a special issue on Jacques Derrida, edited by Marie-Louise Mallet and Ginette Michaud.

PHILOSOPHY IN TURBULENT TIMES

1. GEORGES CANGUILHEM

{A PHILOSOPHY OF HEROISM}

IN THE LAST ARTICLE HE APPROVED FOR PUBLICATION, TWO months before dying, Michel Foucault expressed his deep respect for Georges Canguilhem, emphasizing the position he had held in the history of philosophy in France:

> This man, whose oeuvre was austere, narrowly bounded by choice, and carefully focused on a particular area within the history of science—which is not, in any case, regarded as a spectacular discipline—still found himself involved, to a certain extent, in debates in which he himself was careful never to intervene. But screen out Canguilhem and you will not be able to make much sense of a whole series of discussions among French Marxists; you will fail to grasp the specific factors that make sociologists like Bourdieu, Castel and Passeron so eminent in their field; and you will miss a whole aspect of the theoretical work done by psychoanalysts, particularly the Lacanians. More than that: across the spectrum of intellectual debate that preceded and followed the movement of

1968, it is easy to tell which participants had been formed, at first-hand or remotely, by Canguilhem.[1]

Foucault added that *The Normal and the Pathological* was without doubt his most significant book.[2] It conveyed, he said, the essence of Canguilhem's work: reflection on life and death; valorization of the status of "error" and rationality in the history of science; insistence on the notions of continuity and rupture, norm and anomaly; and a thoroughly modern view of the relationship between experimentation and conceptualization in the field of medicine.

Pursuing this theme, Foucault pointed to the fault line separating two main currents of contemporary thought in France: on one hand a philosophy of experience, of sense, and of the subject (the line running from Merleau-Ponty to Sartre), and on the other a philosophy of knowledge, rationality, and conceptuality (Cavaillès, Canguilhem, Koyré). The second of these, apparently more speculative and remote from any form of subjective and political commitment, was the one that had taken part in the struggle against the Nazis. No doubt the author of *History of Madness* had himself in mind in saluting the courage of a man who had been a hero of the Resistance before becoming Foucault's own master.[3] Was Foucault himself not also an austere historian of science engaged in a political struggle, not against fascism but against more subtle forms of oppression?

In truth, Canguilhem himself had already pointed out this fault line previously, once in 1943, when he defended his thesis on the normal and the pathological while risking his life as a resister; and again in 1976, when he composed a eulogy for his friend Jean Cavaillès, who had been killed by the Nazis: "His mathematical philosophy was not constructed with reference to any Subject that might momentarily and precariously be identified with Jean Cavaillès. This philosophy, from which Jean Cavaillès is radically absent, dictated a form of action that led him, along the narrow paths of logic, to that crossing from which none return. Jean Cavaillès was the logic of the Resistance lived out right up to death. Let the philosophers of existence and of the person do as well the next time around, if they can."[4] Canguilhem was pointing to a logical coherence, grounded in the primacy of the concept, between political commitment and intellectual activity. Foucault, nineteen years later, was emphasizing a caesura between a commitment in the service of liberty and the fact of defending a philosophy of the concept. Yet in 1983 he himself echoed Canguilhem's idea of logical coherence: "One of the French philosophers who engaged in the Resistance during the war was Cavaillès, a historian of mathematics who worked on the development of its internal structure. No philosopher of political commitment, not Sartre, not Simone de Beauvoir, not Merleau-Ponty, made any effort at all."[5] If such a dialectic is present in the positing of a foundational relation between, on one hand, a philosophy of liberty and the subject, and on the other, a philosophy of concept and structure, that perhaps signifies that these are the two major paradigms that govern, in originary fashion, the relationship between a politics and a philosophy. But one might then maintain that only when the Freudian concept of the unconscious (irreducible as it is to any psychology of the person) is introduced does it become possible to resolve and overcome this contradiction.

Like many of his generation who studied at the École Normale Superieure (ENS), Canguilhem was a pure product of the educational system of the Third Republic. He was born on 4 June 1904 at Castelnaudary into a milieu of petit-bourgeois artisans; his father was the village tailor and his forebears were peasants from the south of France. Throughout his life he retained a local accent that gave his voice a particular resonance, at once blunt and determined. When he was ten he learned how to work the land on the farm his mother had inherited at Orgibet, on the border between the Aude and Ariège regions, land he himself managed during the period between the wars. He was a brilliant pupil in his native city before moving to Paris, where in 1921 he became a *khâgneux* at a distinguished upper secondary school, the lycée Henri-IV. Traditional student argot gave (and gives) the name *khâgneux* (= *cagneux*, or wretches) to students in the humanities division, technically known as the division of higher rhetoric, of the preparatory course (*khâgne*) for the ENS. The science students for their part got the nickname *taupins*, which suggests subterranean labor (*taupe*, literally "mole," is a term for a mining engineer).[6]

The dominant figure at the lycée Henri-IV was Émile Chartier, better known under the pseudonym "Alain." A student of Jules Lagneau, Alain succeeded Henri Bergson, Victor Delbos, and Léon Brunschvicg as a *khâgne* instructor. He had been a supporter of Dreyfus, and when the war came had volunteered for duty in the front lines, refusing to assume officer rank. Horrified by the mass slaughter of World War One, he had become convinced that philosophy must not stand apart from political thought. Hence he adopted a stance of radical pacifism, allied to a moderate humanism. A remarkable speaker, Alain was able to awaken the critical spirit of the youthful elite of the nation without claiming to impose any system of thought on them. For many years (until 1933) he passed on to them his ideal of a philosophy of action, deliberately Voltairean and grounded in the primacy of freedom, of the moral conscience, and of reason. In 1921 he began publishing *Libres Propos* with Gallimard. The weekly journal, some twenty pages in length to which many of his students contributed, served as a vehicle for his radicalism, his pacifism, and his hostility to the institutional military.

The young Canguilhem became a devotee of Alain. When he was admitted to the ENS in 1924, thus becoming a *normalien*, his classmates included Jean-Paul Sartre, Paul Nizan, Daniel Lagache, and Raymond Aron. Two years later, tutored by Célestin Bouglé, he took his diploma of higher studies at the Sorbonne for his work on "the theory of order and progress in Auguste Comte." In 1927 he achieved the *agrégation* in philosophy, becoming a qualified instructor at the higher secondary and university levels. In the same year he began to publish articles in *Libres Propos* under the pseudonym C. G. Bernard.

In 1927 Canguilhem, an ardent pacifist, took a leading part in the student protest movement against the established order within the ENS. For the school's annual revue, he and his friend Sylvain Broussaudier staged a show entitled *Le désastre de Langson*. In it, the name of the prestigious director of the ENS, Gustave Lanson, the author of a well-known manual of literary history, was linked with a rather inglorious episode of the French conquest of Indochina, the battle of Lang Son in the 1880s. In two numbers, part satire and part prank, the authors heaped scorn on the French army, especially on one article of a law passed by the French parliament the same year that stipulated that in time of war the government should take all necessary measures *"dans l'ordre intellectuel"* to maintain national morale. The most scandalous part came when the actors sang, to the tune of "La Marseillaise," verses from the *Complainte du capitaine Cambusat* in which the military instructors of the ENS were severely ridiculed.

Vexed by these attacks, Gustave Lanson reprimanded the perpetrators of the prank and forwarded a file on them to the war ministry. Accused of revolutionary propaganda, the pacifist *normaliens* signed a petition the following year against the advanced military training they were compelled to receive. Canguilhem found a way to protest by letting the tripod of a machine gun fall and hit his instructor, thus choosing deliberately to fail as an officer-in-training. This earned him eighteen months of military service with the rank of corporal.[7]

From 1930 on, pacifism in the manner of Alain gradually became irrelevant. The former *khâgne* students of the lycée Henri-IV turned to new commitments. The economic crisis and the rise of fascism thrust them into an environment very different from that of their youth. Nevertheless, after being appointed to a teaching post at Charleville, Georges Canguilhem repeatedly demonstrated that he had kept faith with the teaching of Émile Chartier, especially in supporting the "integral pacifism" of Félicien Challaye, a professor at the lycée Condorcet and in declaring himself hostile to all forms of established power, in the name of Socratic citizenship.[8] Starting in 1934, though, he realized that Hitler's rise to power had rendered his former antimilitary revolt pointless. After having taught at Albi, Douai, and Valenciennes, he joined Paul Langevin and Paul Rivet on the Vigilance Committee of antifascist intellectuals, which Alain and Challaye had also joined.[9]

The nations had gone to war against one another in 1914 in order to safeguard the interests of the ruling classes and the empires, to the detriment of peoples and individuals who held to the Enlightenment ideal of a Europe without national homelands or borders. In the coming war, the forces of tolerance were ranging themselves against those of tyranny, and it was impossible to view the outcome in the same light, given that the nations were about to clash not as such but in the name of liberty against slavery. In this new context, support of pacifism could mean abdication in the face of the destructive power incarnated by Hitler and his allies. The choice of Canguilhem, and those who followed the same trajectory, was thus similar in nature to, and anticipated, their subsequent decision to reject first the Munich pact, and then the handshake between Marshal Pétain and Hitler at Montoire in October 1940.

In October 1936, after a year spent in Béziers, Canguilhem was appointed to Toulouse, and became in turn a professor in charge of a *khâgne*. Though he now assumed the mantle of his own former master, the new instructor could not have been more different from Alain in the classroom. Classical and severe, he soon adopted the bearing of a cavalry officer, incarnating to the point of ascesis all the virtues of republican schooling. His students at Toulouse were inculcated with a sense of order, logic, and discipline, as their teacher laid down a series of prohibitions in the classroom: no notebooks, no pencils, a refusal even to allow certain expressions to be uttered. The normal method was for the students to take lecture notes, thus fixing the knowledge transmitted in permanent form; Canguilhem preferred them to assemble flexible archives, grouped into thematic dossiers or adaptable modules.

Similarly, in order to exercise the critical faculty of his pupils and train them to develop an intelligent memory, he forced them to write down and submit summaries of what they had heard in class after an hour of attentive listening during which they took no notes. The summaries were neither returned nor commented upon. Canguilhem never advocated the sort of pedagogy that puts student and teacher on the same level, and he never yielded to the temptations of false freedom of speech: his preference was for dictating or mimeographing his courses.[10] The man who had challenged authority in the most radical fashion was the same man who, in his classroom, required the greatest submission from his students, as he imparted knowledge to them in a manner seemingly remote from any practice of liberty. José Cabanis wrote: "For me, Canguilhem's class in the lycée was not the discovery [of] a truth, but of a method, to which I don't believe I have been unfaithful: a critical reflection that takes nothing for granted, takes its distance, and assesses the concrete evidence, while at the same time it intimately espouses, slips stealthily, to the heart of the matter to know it better: at once embrace, retreat, and vigilance."[11] From his years as a pacifist Canguilhem had thus retained not a love of revolt or opposition, but the very essence of their deep causality: a true spirit of resistance, grounded in the effectiveness of prohibition and authority. Every man ought, in his view, to be a rebel, but every rebellion ought to aim at the creation of an order higher than that of subjective liberty: an order of reason and conceptuality.

During this period Canguilhem decided to undertake the study of medicine. Philosophers who adopted a similar course usually did so because they were interested in psychopathology and the treatment of mental illness—Pierre Janet for example. Their purpose was to develop the field of clinical psychology and thus to transform psychiatric knowledge in a dynamic fashion, even to detach it completely from the medical profession. Canguilhem stood apart, for he never saw himself as belonging to this tradition. As a youth he had been exposed, like all the *normaliens* of his generation, to the famous presentations of mentally ill patients by Georges Dumas, but these had left him unimpressed.

So by choosing medicine Canguilhem did appear to be turning away from philosophy, but not down a well-trodden path. It may be that he was experiencing a certain disappointment with philosophy, as he himself said. The truth of the matter is no doubt more complex. He was a man of action, born to a rural family and responsive to manual gesticulation and to the work of farming the land, so much so that he took a keen interest in the agricultural crisis under the Nazi and fascist regimes. His choice was a way of confronting a concrete experience, a "terrain," a discipline that, while not scientific, made it possible to give body and life to conceptual thought. Medicine had been left to its own devices a hundred years previously by philosophy, both because it had no place among the so-called noble sciences like mathematics and physics, and also because of its convergence with biology, likewise the object of philosophical disdain. So it offered the young philosopher the challenge of a new form of rationality.

As Michel Foucault points out, the history of science owed its dignity to the fact that, beginning in the eighteenth century, it had forced the high intellectual tradition to face the question of its own foundation, its rights, its powers, and the conditions of its own practice. And in the first quarter of the twentieth century this interrogation had acquired massive importance in philosophy with the publication of the works of Edmund Husserl.

The German philosopher's theses began to become known in France starting in the 1920s, especially after February 1929, when he delivered the famous lectures entitled *Cartesian Meditations* before the French Philosophical Society.[12] With Descartes's *cogito* as its basis, Husserlian phenomenology affirmed that there is no certain knowledge outside of *my* existence as a thinking being. Hence the notion of phenomenological reduction, which posits the primacy of the ego and of thought, and goes beyond so-called natural experience to attain a vision of existence as consciousness of the world. The ego thus becomes transcendental and consciousness intentional, since it "aims at" something. Thus the sense of the other is formed in the ego, out of a series of experiences. Transcendental intersubjectivity is then defined as a reality against which the ego of every individual figures in relief.

In 1935, in *The Crisis of European Sciences and Transcendental Phenomenology* Husserl demonstrated that the quest for this intersubjectivity could preserve the human sciences from inhumanity.[13] In other words, transcendental phenomenology, by shielding the ego from scientific formalism, was saving a potential science of man in which the ego could be discovered as a consequence of the living being, or as life itself. Thus, faced with mounting barbarity and its threat to world peace, Husserl appealed to a European philosophical conscience, one responding to a humanity desiring to live in the free construction of its own existence.

Husserl's oeuvre could in fact be apprehended in two different ways. Read in light of Nietzsche, and subsequently Heidegger, it allowed a critique of the ideal of progress proper to the Enlightenment and a situating of the weakness of being at the heart of the subject, thus yielding a new philosophy of sense and the subject. But in another perspective, albeit one that does not exclude the first, it opened the way to a possible philosophy of knowledge from which any form of ontological or psychological subject would be evacuated.[14] The first way was taken by Sartre and Merleau-Ponty; the second, by Alexandre Koyré and Canguilhem. Jacques Lacan, it is worth noting, would choose a middle way between these two orientations, defending both a theory of the subject and a form of rationality dependent on unconscious determination.

Although the reference to Husserl's oeuvre is present in all Canguilhem's thinking, it was not through it that he made his mark on the history of science on the eve of World War Two. In preference to this royal road, he chose the paths of medicine on one hand and technology on the other. As a participant in the tricentennial commemoration of Descartes's *Discourse on Method*, he gave a paper in 1937 that bore witness to this evolution, as did the course he gave the following year. He showed that the sciences always arise within a setting in which a transformation of technologies has preceded them. Thus the scientist intervenes merely to make explicit, purify, or clarify a knowledge empirical in origin. As for conceptualization, it draws its capacity to emerge from reflective thinking that concentrates less on observing technological success than on reviewing the attempts that, for unknown reasons, failed.[15]

In 1939, foreseeing the storm that was about to batter Europe, Canguilhem cowrote a work with his comrade Camille Planet in which he took leave for good of the pacifist ideals of his youth: "As for the position of those who value peace above all else, whatever its generosity of inspiration and whatever the soundness of the arguments it advances, it does suffer from this defect: that which it calls peace remains a purely verbal negation of war. In other words, pacifism appears not to recognize that what has been called peace up to now is not the non-existence or annulment of international conflicts, but one form of such conflicts, of which war is only another form."[16] In the last lines of this work, Canguilhem invited the reader to make a clear choice. War, he was saying in essence, is a clash between two types of society, and one must be able to choose which side one is on, like Shakespeare's Hamlet.

In September 1940, just as the new academic year was starting, Canguilhem made his choice. In his eyes, as he was to write later, the military defeat of France was an unacceptable humiliation: "You would need to believe that you were intimately familiar with the paths and purposes of Providence to see this as a promise of moral renewal. And you would need to be greedy indeed for power to see this as the occasion for political regeneration or social revolution."[17] Since he refused to obey Marshal Pétain, Canguilhem decided to resign from the French university system for "personal reasons." To Robert Deltheil, rector of the Academy of Toulouse, he declared: "I did not pass my agrégation in philosophy in order to teach Work, Family, and Homeland."[18]

His wife, Simone, who kept her job as a teacher and her salary, supported him and their three young children while her husband devoted himself to the study of medicine. Meanwhile Jean-Pierre Vernant, the future hero of the communist Resistance under the cover name "Colonel Berthier," took his place in the *khâgne* in Toulouse. Canguilhem's retirement was brief. In February 1941 Jean Cavaillès, a lecturer in logic and philosophy at the University of Strasbourg, which had been relocated to Clermont-Ferrand, was named to the Sorbonne, and he succeeded in convincing his friend to take his place. At the same time he invited Canguilhem to join the Resistance movement that was being organized in the Auvergne region. So Canguilhem returned to teaching, while participating, along with Émmanuel d'Astier de la Vigerie, in the activities of the Libération movement (later to become Libération-Sud).

In the Maquis Canguilhem's cover name was Lafont. He worked closely with Henry Ingrand, one of the leaders of the Resistance in the Auvergne.[19] At the same time, he was pursuing his work as a university instructor and researcher. In 1941–42 he discovered the work of Kurt Goldstein while auditing a course given by his friend Daniel Lagache. In July 1943, having accomplished a considerable quantity of research despite the difficulties of wartime, he defended his doctoral thesis in medicine before a board headed by Alfred Schwarz, a professor of pharmacology and experimental medicine, on the topic of the normal and the pathological. He had already given a course on this topic, which he had studied with members of the Strasbourg faculty, especially the physiologist Charles Kayser and the histologist Marc Klein.

Nothing in this magisterial text allowed the reader the slightest glimpse of the author's alter ego as Lafont. The gap between the brilliant hypotheses of the philosopher and the external context, which is completely absent from his reasoned prose, was so wide that it is still hard to believe, even today, that a thesis of this kind could have been defended in wartime, and at a moment when, with the collapse of the Axis powers in Africa and the Allied landing in Italy, the defeat of fascism in Europe was on the horizon. And yet the intellectual inquiry of the philosopher was not alien to the activities of the Maquisard. It should be noted that Canguilhem was never, like Cavaillès, a military combatant, prepared to use small arms to inflict deadly force. From his days as a pacifist he had retained a distaste for physical violence; no doubt he had become a pacifist on account of the repulsion he felt for the furious impetus of war.

The fact is that his role in the Maquis was essentially humanitarian: he practiced clandestine medicine, at the risk of his life.[20] Indeed, this was the only period of his existence during which he worked as a physician and surgeon. In other words, he was a medical doctor exclusively during the war, and because of the war: an emergency doctor treating wounds and severe injuries, a doctor amid sudden and immediate realities, amid the rush and the trauma of events. He never practiced medicine again afterward, and he declined to register with the *ordre des médecins*, the organization of medical professionals.

From this perspective, medicine and the Resistance were entirely co-involved in the itinerary that led to his brilliant destiny as the man who endowed the concept of normality with new meaning. If commencing the study of medicine allowed the philosopher Canguilhem to become Lafont, that was because the Resistance, as a singular form of rebellion, functioned for him as the paradigm of a discontinuity in the order of normativity, that is to say, as the moment of the adoption of a new norm, issuing from life. Here one inevitably thinks of Nietzsche's affirmation that only adhesion to the force of the present gives one the right to interrogate the past, so as to better understand the future. It is impossible to overemphasize that the simultaneous lived experience of two modalities of a philosophy of action—the act of resistance, the act of caregiving—inspired Canguilhem's thinking about the nature of normality.

What was normality in June 1940? Was it submission to an order accepted by almost an entire people and incarnated by a man declaring that he was making a gift of his own person to France? Or was it, on the contrary, the choice of another norm, a radical break with the appearance of normality offering few prospects, in the short term, of anything other than exile or death? Where exactly did the norm lie in that decisive moment? In London? In the Maquis? At Vichy?

Canguilhem's response to this question, in company with a few other intellectuals, helped to save France not just from slavery and military defeat but even more from dishonor and humiliation. Some paid for it with their lives—Marc Bloch, Albert Lautmann, Boris Vildé, Georges Politzer—while others survived to bear witness: Jean-Pierre Vernant, Lucie and Raymond Aubrac. Canguilhem shared their luck. And throughout his life he made a point of reminding younger generations of those who had sacrificed their future in the cause of liberty. He was always able to find the words to say that no norm arising out of life, or better still no norm that included death in the process of life, could ever justify preferring Pétain to de Gaulle, fascism to antifascism, Pierre Laval to Jean Moulin. A hero becomes a hero and dies so that life may continue, because he has understood this message, through which death always demands a reckoning from life. And in this sense too, a hero is distinct from a fanatic or a terrorist.[21] At a time like the one we are living through now, when it is fashionable to travesty the heroes of the Resistance and depict them as morally deficient or even abject—I am thinking especially of the attacks on Jean Moulin and Raymond Aubrac[22]—it is worth remembering that no challenge to hagiography or legend can justify abolishing the very essence of heroism.

It is Homer's *Iliad* that gives us the most compelling definition of heroism, at the moment when each of the protagonists of the future tragedy of war is confronted with his destiny. And as readers know, only Achilles shows himself capable of incarnating the absolute ideal of "a beautiful death and a short life" that lies at the origin of the Greek concept of heroism.[23] For Achilles, the man of short life and glorious death, is not just the only one who always leads in combat, never hesitating for an instant to put his life on the line; he is also the one who, in making this choice, has already renounced, in advance and unconditionally, the ordinary honor of earthly sovereignty for the sake of the heroic honor of immortality. He prefers to lose his life so as to become a legend rather than garner the rewards of victory some day when peace has returned. Achilles thus resolves, as Jean-Pierre Vernant explains, one of the great enigmas of the human condition: "To find in death the means to overcome it, to conquer death through death itself, in giving it the meaning it does not have, of which it is absolutely bare."[24]

Canguilhem was of course sufficiently acquainted with Greek literature not to be unfamiliar with the lesson of the *Iliad*. But he was fascinated by the decision to take concrete action, which, in an intellectual, characterizes the choice of a heroic destiny. He often pondered the problem of the moment at which a thinker engaged in intellectual work can make a commitment to action that may cost him the sacrifice, not just of his life in order to vanquish death but also the future of the work that he bears inside him. Heroism in this case assumes the courage to choose the beautiful death and the short life, but it is more than just that.

What would the oeuvre of Marc Bloch and Jean Cavaillès have been if they had not fallen in action? And vice versa, what would have been Georges Canguilhem's place in French philosophy if he had met death in the Maquis before he had drafted a single line of the works that lay ahead? When one thinks of Boris Vildé, torn from life before he could fulfill his destiny as an ethnologist, one can't help posing this question. And Canguilhem did pose it. I can testify to that.

Heroism, he used to say, is a manner of conceiving of action under the category of a universal, from which the psychological subject in any form is excluded. Once the decision is made, once the encounter between the history of an individual and the history of the world has come about, things proceed as if every step ahead, every gesture, were imposed from outside, with no direction or premeditation. "Action is always the offspring of rigor before it is the sister of dream."[25] The force of this definition, which, with Canguilhem, is valid essentially for an intellectual, lies in the fact that it relates every heroic act to the almost unconscious, but deliberately chosen, rigor of the act itself.

Of course a man can always invoke his past, his "roots," his particular history as the cause of his decision, as Jean-Pierre Vernant did: "In 1940, at the moment of defeat, it was my own roots that I felt, so deeply that I said to myself that living with this German and Nazi occupation was out of the question. And yet, when the war in Algeria arose, the same fellow, the same Frenchman, with the same feeling of fidelity to his own identity, took the view that the Algerians had the right to be independent, and that in terms of my own particularist nationalist tradition, I couldn't not acknowledge the same rights in others that I had defended myself when the Germans were in my country."[26] This example shows, however, that the act of resisting, which engages the essence of heroism, depends on something quite different from attachment to a landscape, its traditions, its gastronomy, or the beauty of its countryside. If, for the *same* reasons, the *same* man can wish to save France from the shame imposed by Nazism and Algeria from the colonial servitude imposed by France, it is because the decision to act operates in the name of a universal—or more exactly, in the name of a shedding of the ego and an access to the truth of the self—which goes far beyond the reference to particularism. *Taking action* then depends on the proper identity of a man (and thus of the human in general) and on his capacity to fuse with action itself, in the present instant: "If I get out of this," wrote René Char, "I know that I will have to break with the aroma of these essential years, reject (not repress) my treasure silently, far from me."[27]

Consequently it matters little whether the hero is a simple soldier landing at dawn on a beach in Normandy, or a philosopher, a mathematician, and Spinozist, capable of grasping that will and understanding are one and the same thing. It matters little whether he is a militant or a civil servant refusing to talk under torture, or a secret agent, donning many masks. In short, little importance attaches to the prior or future being of the hero, his "psychological case," his social origin, or what he tells himself are the reasons for his choice. The only thing that counts in heroism is the destiny chosen—that of Achilles—that commands the instantaneous rigor of the act and guides it to its incandescence. For action then becomes a work. Rimbaud said that spiritual combat is just as brutal as physical battle between men.

No doubt Canguilhem would have composed his inaugural book— *The Normal and the Pathological*—in the same way if the historical circumstances had been different. No doubt he would have found the same wording and the same concepts in peacetime. But had that been the case, would this major work have achieved the greatness it did? Would it have occupied the same place in the eyes of a whole generation of philosophers and intellectuals? Would it have permitted all those who were later to cite it to understand that the reversal of the notion of "the norm" carried out by the author was as much a way of disengaging from any psychology of the subject as it was of creating a new philosophy of heroism grounded in the rigor of a conceptual analysis?

The definition of normality and pathology furnished by Canguilhem in the preface of the book is well known: "Pathological phenomena are identical to normal phenomena, except for quantitative variations."[28] It was identical to that advanced by Lacan in 1932 in his thesis in medicine on paranoid psychosis.[29] In both cases it was a question, for biological as for psychical and mental questions, of embracing in a single essence, defining their dissonance, the states of mind [*affections*] called normal and the ones labeled pathological. In this conception, psychosis (as mental disturbance) and illness (as organic disturbance) are no longer comparable to fixed constitutions, but reactions of the body or the personality to a life situation.

In thinking this problematic, Lacan had relied on the philosophy of Spinoza. Canguilhem, ten years later, was inspired by Kurt Goldstein's work *The Structure of the Organism*, published in Germany in 1934.[30] Canguilhem did pay tribute, though, to French psychiatric knowledge, especially to Charles Blondel, Eugène Minkowski, and Daniel Lagache, who themselves had helped to "define the general essence of the morbid or abnormal psychical fact and its relation to the normal."[31]

A psychiatrist and neurologist formed on the battlefields of the great slaughter of 1914–1918, Goldstein had treated victims of brain injury and had observed that the establishment of new norms of life entailed a reduction of the level of their activity in a new but "narrower" setting. This narrowing, in patients suffering from brain injury, resulted from their inability to respond to the requirements of a norm prior to their present state. Narrowing, not regression: the originality of the illness, according to Goldstein, was actually that it did not lead to any reversibility of life. The patients's new state of health is never the same as the former one. As Canguilhem put it, "No recovery is ever a return to biological innocence. To recover is to establish new norms of living for oneself that are occasionally superior to the old ones."[32]

It is well known that the circumstances of wartime reverse the habitual norms of peacetime and make it possible to understand the relation between norm and pathology differently. Like war, illness is an upheaval, an imperiling of existence through which the organism reacts in a catastrophic manner in a setting proper to it. And amid the urgency of war, there is always a doctor ready to supply the patient with devoted care and, as circumstances dictate, to conceive a new theory of the norm. But there are numerous other situations in which the world's violence may cause a new outlook on the normal and the pathological to emerge in the consciousness of a clinician or a scientist, at the risk of his life. In this respect, there is perhaps not all that much difference between an Ambroise Paré, an Ignace Semmelweis, and a Xavier Bichat.

From his war experience Goldstein came to the view that any theory had to be based on a "clinic" issuing from direct observation of the patient (the notion of "individual being"), the only way to construct a phenomenological conception of the organism comprising the relation of the latter to a setting, an environment, a subject.

From the viewpoint both of psychiatry and of neurology, the question was thus the same: it was necessary to think the normal and the pathological together, in order to reestablish the primacy of a subjectivity, meaning an existence reacting to a setting. For Goldstein, as for Canguilhem, the subject is internal to the living being, in Minkowski it is existential—and for Lacan it would be determined by a language.

In the first part of *The Normal and the Pathological* Canguilhem shows that two conceptions of illness are grounded in the idea that the pathological state is only a quantitative modification of the normal state. The modern one, issuing from the work of Pasteur, assimilates the illness to an external agent (microbe or virus) foreign to the body. The other, in the Hippocratic tradition, maintains that the illness intervenes to upset the equilibrium of the humors. On this view the agent is no longer external but internal to the body whose natural harmony it disturbs. The first conception gives rise to an ontological medicine; the second, to a dynamic medicine.

The opposition between these two currents is exemplified in the renowned debate between Auguste Comte and Claude Bernard. Comte took from François Broussais the principle that illness is either a defect, or an excess, of irritation of the various tissues, and he used the pathological as a basis from which to explore the normal. Claude Bernard, seeing the pathological state as an alteration of the normal state, began with the latter to explain the former.

Canguilhem's critical examination of these two positions, which signify the birth of modern scientific medicine, leads him to conclude that Claude Bernard adoped too physiological a view of illness. If physiology is capable of identifying an illness, it is to the clinic that physiological science owes this perceptive capacity. In other words, although physiology may underpin the medical discipline scientifically, only the clinic has the capacity to bring physiology into direct contact with existing individuals. This is why, having focused on the concepts of a philosopher (Comte), then of a scientist (Claude Bernard), Canguilhem studies the art of the clinic as practiced by someone with practical experience, the physician René Leriche.

A direct descendant of Claude Bernard, Leriche sees a continuity between the physiological state (the state of health) and the pathological state. But he considers that physiology is insufficient to explain illness, and that it is illness itself that sheds light on physiology. Leriche thus privileges a dynamic medicine into which the patient's point of view has to be introduced, with her suffering and pain. "Health," Leriche writes, " is the silence of the organs. . . . Illness is that which hinders humans in the normal exercise of their lives . . . and above all, that which makes them suffer."

Canguilhem, after expressing his agreement with Leriche's view, asks in the second part of his book whether there exists a science of the normal and the pathological. It is at this point in his reasoning that he adopts Goldstein's theses, so as to present the patient's point of view as the only one competent to judge normality, and in order to demonstrate that physiology is "the science of the stabilized traits of life" [*la science des allures stabilisées de la vie*]. I note that this superb definition takes its distance from the traditional one of physiology as "the science of the functions of the human body in a state of health."

Canguilhem then distinguishes between anomaly, illness, and pathology. Anomaly is defined in space and without reference to the patient: it breaks out in a "spatial multiplicity." Illness is situated in time and always presupposes the existence of a conscious subject revealing his pain in his interaction with the doctor. It is a property of illness to "break out in chronological succession." But even when it goes from the critical or acute stages to the chronic stage, it leaves its imprint on the body or the consciousness of the patient, like a "once in the past" for which he retains a nostalgia: "Thus one is ill not just with respect to others, but in relation to oneself."[33] As for pathology, it pertains to biology and not to physiology.

In order to explore these definitions fully, Canguilhem undertakes a semantic study of the terms "anomaly," "abnormality," and "normality." "Anomaly" is a substantive for which there is no corresponding adjective in French, and which designates an unusual biological fact unrelated to an abnormality, an illness, or a pathology, but which is linked to a vital *normativity*, meaning to the manner in which life produces its own norms. An anomaly is thus the equivalent of a monstrosity, an infirmity, or an irregularity in the order of biology. It is constitutional or congenital: cyclopia, hermaphrodism, harelip, and so on.[34]

Pathology on the contrary implies a *pathos*, that is to say, a direct and concrete feeling of suffering and powerlessness. It is thus the sign of an abnormality, on condition that abnormality is defined by relative statistical frequency. The abnormal is just as normal as the normal, since both realities depend on the organization of the living being. Uninterrupted perfect health, for example, is seen as an abnormal fact: "The pathological state cannot be called normal without committing an absurdity, inasmuch as it expresses a relation to the normativity of life. But normal in this sense cannot be equated to the physiologically normal without committing an absurdity either, for different norms are in question here. The abnormal is not such through the absence of normality. There is no life without norms of life, and the morbid state is always a certain way of living."[35]

Far from abandoning the terrain of physiology for the subject's straightforward lived experience of illness, Canguilhem locates the clinic in a region close to, or beyond, the limits of consciousness.[36] So the only reason there is a science of pathology is that life itself introduces into human consciousness the categories of life and health. In other words the norm, far from being external to the living being, is produced by the very movement of life. There is, in consequence, no "biological science of the normal. There is a science of the situations and conditions *called* normal. This science is physiology."[37] So physiology is indeed "the science of the stabilized traits of life," and it is indeed physiology that, in origin, grounds the discipline of medicine, but only the clinic gives validity to the concept of pathology. From this the status of modern medicine follows: while not itself a science, it makes use of the results of *all* the sciences in the service of the norms of life. However, if it can only exist because humans feel unwell, it is also thanks to its existence that these same humans are able to know *in what respect* [*en quoi*] and *with what* [*de quoi*] they are ill.

Canguilhem winds up his demonstration with a declaration that gains in prophetic force from the fact that when he wrote, the laboratory did not yet dominate clinical knowledge. He emphasizes that no laboratory experiment (no physiology) will ever have diagnostic value if its goal is to supplant clinical observation. Never was this magisterial declaration more pertinent than it is today! Only a revalorization of the clinical art, based on listening to and observing the patient, can guarantee the practioner of modern medicine a true status and keep him from becoming a valet to the laboratory and pharmacology. For it is certain that both a correct reading of laboratory test results and the capacity to prescribe the right (and thus effective) therapy are dependent on the diagnostic art.

Canguilhem continued to act as the doctor to the Maquis in the Auvergne even after he had defended his thesis, a thesis that was destined to have so much impact on the philosophical generation of the 1960s, on the students of Jacques Lacan and the students of Louis Althusser,[38] on Foucault, on clinicians of every sort, and on historians of science. Early in 1944 he set up a field hospital at Maurines, and during the summer he spent several weeks at the hospital of Saint-Alban, where he concealed and tended to the wounded. The first experiment in institutional psychotherapy was taking place there, in a spirit of antifascism and under the guidance of François Tosquelles and Lucien Bonnafé. At Saint-Alban members of the Resistance, mentally ill individuals, poets and therapists, nurse-attendants, and psychiatrists,[39] all mixed freely: "I took part in some of their work. We engaged in much discussion. I well remember their cordiality."[40]

Canguilhem took part subsequently in the battle of Mont-Mouchet, during the course of which the Resistance forces in the Auvergne joined up with the Army of Liberation. He then returned to the Haute-Loire, where his family was, and subsequently went back to Clermont-Ferrand. From there he was sent to Vichy to represent Ingrand, who had just been named commissioner of the republic. At this time he undertook "certain delicate and still dangerous tasks," the nature of which he never specified.[41] On 12 September 1944 Canguilhem received the Croix de Guerre directly from the minister of war of the time. Did he perhaps recall, at that moment, the reprimand he had received seventeen years earlier, from a previous holder of the office of minister of war?

After the liberation he returned to his teaching duties at the University of Strasbourg. From 1948 to 1955 he held the post of inspector general of philosophy in the Ministry of National Education. In 1955 he defended his doctoral thesis in philosophy, on the formation of the concept of reflex,[42] before succeeding Gaston Bachelard at the Sorbonne as director of the Institute of the History of Science and Technology of the University of Paris. Known to his students and close collaborators as "le Cang," he kept this post until 1971 and was thus able to exercise considerable influence on philosophy students, both through his courses and his books—and in his role as president of the jury of the *agrégation*.

Bertrand Saint-Sernin, one of his students, has left an unforgettable portrait of him:

> He was admired, feared, imitated, loved, but also courted and criticized. He had more social power than his personal ethic warranted, and less immediate influence than he would have had if he had not sometimes constrained his own genius, for mysterious reasons. He judged himself unworthy, as I see it, of the grace that is the life of the mind, and rejected what others took to be the plain fact of his own greatness, because of an unfounded but ineradicable humility. Yet when he was analyzing an author, or when he was helping

a student or a researcher to figure out where his interests and talents really lay, something he did with unflagging courteousness, he manifested a flair at once vital and spiritual.[43]

Canguilhem's principal work, written while the war was raging, had four successive editions.[44] The first, published at Clermont-Ferrand in 1943, bore the title *Essay on Some Problems Regarding the Normal and the Pathological*. This version was republished with a new preface in 1950. Only in 1966 did Canguilhem make major alterations to the text, giving it the simpler title *The Normal and the Pathological* and adding a note to the reader and a new chapter, both of which were written between 1963 and 1966. The new chapter was organized into three parts ("From the Social to the Vital," "On organic Norms in Man," and "A New Concept in Pathology: Error"). As for the note to the reader, its title, "Twenty Years Later," referred to a heroic, indeed Homeric, epic.[45] Canguilhem added greater nuance to some of his assessments of Claude Bernard, in whom he now detected a concern for the clinic that had escaped him in 1943. Correspondingly, he cast a slightly colder glance at Leriche. For the last edition, which appeared in 1972, Canguilhem took care to add an appendix entitled "Detailed Rectifications and Some Complementary Notes." In sum, he continually modified his inaugural work over the course of thirty years. It was as though, at each turning point, he felt impelled to bring it into line with the ethic of reversal of the norm that had marked its origin so strongly.

The boldest alterations, however, the ones made in 1966, can be attributed to Canguilhem's reading of Michel Foucault's *The Birth of the Clinic*.[46] Foucault and Canguilhem had met in 1960. At that time Foucault had asked Canguilhem to act as rapporteur for a thesis in philosophy that was destined to attract a great deal of attention: *Madness and Unreason: A History of Madness in the Classic Age*.[47] Canguilhem understood right away that Foucault had launched a radical revision of the psychiatric mode of thinking about madness and that he was proposing a new way of defining the norm as a historical construct, linked to social normativity and arising out of a tenebrous division between reason and unreason. Canguilhem saw straightaway that it was his reading of the works of

Freud that had enabled Foucault to perceive when and how psychiatry had cut loose from its moorings in philanthropy and transformed itself into a policing of the mad. What Foucault had taken from Freud was not his conception of the norm, but a new way of looking at the structure of the asylum.

In *Birth of the Clinic*, Foucault went further in the same direction, attributing a historical origin to the constitution of modern medicine. For him, modern medicine was born out of the institution of a "medical gaze" constructed as a norm and structured around three nodes. At one of them Foucault situated the patient, likened to an object being looked at, or "object of the gaze." At another node he placed the doctor, who alone was capable of being a "subject of the gaze." The third element was the institution charged with legitimating socially the relation between the gazing subject and the object gazed upon. For Canguilhem's concept of a norm produced by life, Foucault therefore substituted the idea of a norm constructed by the social order and itself the bearer of normalization. In other words, he set a social normativity against a biological normativity, an archaeology against a phenomenology.

The finest pages of his book were devoted to Xavier Bichat, the surgeon known for the dissection of cadavers, who had invented a new conception of the relation between life and death in the midst of the revolutionary upheaval. In dissecting the bodies that were at his disposal on the field of battle, or that he dug up in cemeteries, Bichat had of course believed that he was rediscovering an anatomical-pathological clinic already known. But in carrying out this procedure, he was actually replacing the static cartography of the old order of things with a new principle that purged medical knowledge of its former metaphysics. He was transforming the classical conception of death by depriving the theologians of the divine privilege of belonging. For if life is the ensemble of functions that resist death, that means that God is dispossessed of his right of life and death over the human and animal worlds. Death no longer belongs to him, and it is no longer upon him—neither upon heaven nor upon hell—that the passage from life to death depends, but upon a double process, physiological and pathological, proper to living organisms. Death is thus inscribed in the history of life, as illness is inscribed in the existence of every subject—a symptom, as it were, of death's advance into life. Death, the progressive phenomenon of the slow degradation of bodies, has man in its grip from the moment of his birth, and inhabits him throughout his life, down to the final passage. Gilles Deleuze wrote: "When Foucault analyzes the theses of Bichat, the very tone tells us with sufficient clarity that we are dealing with something other than an epistemological analysis. It is a question of conceiving death, and few men as much as Foucault died in the manner that he conceived death. This power of life that belonged to Foucault, Foucault always thought it and lived it as a multiple death, in the manner of Bichat."[48]

In the period from 1963 to 1966 Canguilhem took on board the Foucauldian substitution of a social normativity for biological normativity, not to disown his thesis of 1943 but to give it a rigor that it would doubtless never have attained without the challenge launched by Foucault—a challenge that Foucault himself had grasped when he was struck by the gesture of Bichat.

While not surrendering the view that the norm has its genesis in the vital forces, Canguilhem now maintained that it could not constitute itself outside the contemplation of its own negativity. Hence the idea that the threat of illness would, for the normal man, be the putting of his health to the test and one of the constituents of human health in general. In sum, Canguilhem sketched the contours of a science of the normal in which the priority of the infraction over regularity, of pathology over normality would have their place alongside the integration in the living being of the dialectic between norm and pathology.

Renouncing in part the vitalist ideals of his youth, as the patient renounces the euphoria of his former state, he assigned man a paradoxical status, that of being in some sense permanently afflicted with "the illness of the normal man." This was his term for "the disturbance that springs from the persistence of the normal state, from the incorruptible uniformity of the normal, the illness that arises from the privation of illness, from an existence almost incompatible with illness. . . . [And he concluded:] It needs, not the first sign of illness but the casting of the shadow of illness, for the normal man to believe and tell himself that that is what he is."[49]

In Canguilhem's revision we can detect both the "cast shadow" of the work of Foucault and a reading of Freud's *Beyond the Pleasure Principle*,[50] a book to which the philosopher continually referred in his subsequent work on the knowledge of life.[51] Canguilhem's Freud was different from Foucault's, no doubt—a more biological Freud, not a destroyer of norms, but the theoretician of the death wish.

It is hard not to see this dialogue between the two men—one attached to a vitalist conception of the phenomena of life and death, the other haunted by a tenebrous cleavage between deathly tyranny and its impossible transgression—as one of the high points of French philosophy in the postwar period. And one of the most unusual, for it is rare to observe such an inversion of filiation, with the master adapting his theory in light of the work of the person who has chosen to become his pupil. Canguilhem put it this way in 1991:

> Thirty years already. Since 1961 other books by Foucault, *The Birth of the Clinic*, *Words and Things: An Archaeology of the Human Sciences*, *A History of Sexuality*, have to some degree eclipsed the initial influence of the *History of Madness*. I admire the first two. I have stated in *The Normal and the Pathological* how much I was moved by the first. For the second I wrote an article that has earned me nothing but approbation. But for me, 1961 remains, and will remain, the year in which a truly great philosopher revealed himself. I already knew at least two, who had been my schoolmates, Raymond Aron and Jean-Paul Sartre. They could be fierce toward one another, and they could be fierce toward Michel Foucault. It did happen, though, that all three were seen together one day: it was to support an enterprise without frontiers, against death.[52]

The composition of Canguilhem's thesis on the normal and the pathological had been carried out at the same time as he was participating in the great struggle of the Resistance. Now it is interesting to note that the whole body of his oeuvre bears the trace of this initial encounter between a philosophy of concepts and a philosophy of commitment. A paradoxical and unexpected trace: for if Canguilhem was never the theorist of a philosophy of subjective commitment, he remained, throughout his life and in the manner of Spinoza, a philosopher of rebellion—conceptual rebellion. That is why he regarded psychology, to the extent that it is the discipline of behavior, adaptation, and conditioning, as a school of submission and of the suppression of liberty. For just as he had always rejected the thought of Taine and that of adepts of theories about native soil, race, and environment, he likewise abhorred any approach to mankind that aimed to reduce the spirit to a thing, the psyche to physiological determinism, thought to a reflex; in sum, the human being to an insect.

This is the background to the famous lecture he delivered on 18 December 1956 before the College of Philosophy, in which he tore into psychology in the most scathing manner, denouncing it as a "philosophy without rigor," because eclectic while posing as objective; as an "undemanding ethics," assembling experiments without critical judgment; and finally as a "medicine with no control," basing its hypotheses on the observation of illnesses that it never succeeded in rendering intelligible: illnesses of the nerves.[53]

After this initial onslaught, Canguilhem showed that the discipline's absence of identity corresponded to an absence of object. And the proof of this lack lay, as far as he was concerned, in the fact that psychology was endlessly hunting for its own impossible unity, that is to say, for an unfindable synthesis among its supposed fields of investigation: experimental psychology, psychoanalysis, clinical psychology, social psychology, and ethnology. As a substitute for this evanescent unity, what one found, according to Canguilhem, was a pact of peaceful coexistence among professionals in constant opposition: masters of submission. A "thing" without essence and without object, psychology thus came down in his eyes to nothing more than a technology at the service of a corporation, itself under the sway of judges, censors, and educators whose function was the instrumentalization of man by man.

Canguilhem did not stop at this congeries of negative definitions. He appealed to history to ground his line of reasoning, and the result was a second death sentence for psychology. Whatever the system of thought upon which it relies in order to ensure its own survival, he explained, it always remains imitative, or is supplanted by another model of intelligibility, or else drowns in its own morass.

When it poses as a science of nature it remains dependent, and has done ever since antiquity, on physiology on one hand and medicine on the other. Thus it is that, as physiology, it was capable of being integrated into the Aristotelian system, in which the soul is treated as the form of the living body and not as a substance separate from matter. As medicine, on the contrary, it was rendered null in the doctrine of Galen, who made the brain the seat of the soul. Thus it has never had a place, since it tried to be the science of two drifting objects.

And when psychology did finally believe that its hour had come, when it posed as the science of subjectivity after the decline of Aristotelian physics, all it did was to take yet another stride toward its own ruin. One moment it fancied itself the physics of the external senses in search of an experimental description of sensation—and all it could do was to imitate mechanistic physics. The next it presented itself as the science of the internal sense, and quickly shrank to being a pedagogy of learning. And in a third phase it constructed itself as a science of the intimate, but then found itself overshadowed on one hand by psychiatry, a branch of medicine, and on the other by psychoanalysis, the only discipline capable of rethinking the principle of consciousness as a function of the notion of the unconscious.

Psychology still had the possibility of constituting itself as a science of behavior and reactions. But this route too, according to Canguilhem, is almost certainly leading to an impasse. Because psychology then leans on biology for support, at the risk of making itself into "the instrument of an ambition to treat man as an instrument." And it drowns in test protocols, assessments, and selection procedures.

Having reduced psychology to a doubly instrumental project, Canguilhem preferred an image that soon became famous because of its very ambiguity, and that generations of psychiatrists, psychologists, and psychoanalysts would comment on: "When you leave the Sorbonne by the rue Saint-Jacques, you can turn uphill or down. If you head uphill, you approach the Pantheon, which is the resting place of various great men;

if you head downhill, you are inevitably on your way to police head-quarters."[54] What the philosopher meant was, psychology was always condemned to try in vain to liken itself to a philosophy of heroism, while ceaselessly putting into operation a technology of submission.

So why was Canguilhem so eager, in 1956, to denounce this false science, which as far as he was concerned had neither object nor identity? Why such violence? Was psychology really such a threatening presence in the postwar French university system that one of the greatest philosophers of the century felt compelled to display such detestation of it?

What Canguilhem was really attacking in 1956 was the project of his former schoolmate and friend at the ENS, Daniel Lagache, who was attempting both to unify the various branches of psychology and to introduce the teaching of the psychoanalytic clinic into the discipline. In this "unitary" program Canguilhem perceived a danger taking shape—that of the subjection of the noble disciplines (medicine, biology, physiology, philosophy, literature, etc.) to a model of instrumentalization of the spirit and the psyche, which might in the long term transform the teachers and professors of the French republic into psycho-pedagogues more concerned with aiding students in distress than with forming elites in the service of an ideal of liberty. In Canguilhem's view this model also threatened, given the formidable expansion of the study of psychology in the democratic countries, to contaminate the whole of the social edifice, to the point where the business of managing interpersonal relationships would supplant all forms of political and intellectual commitment.

For this reason he displayed a special virulence toward behavioral psychology,[55] fearing, not without reason, that it would succeed in imposing its sovereignty on the other branches of psychology by reason of the scientistic claims it was advancing, despite the courageous struggle that clinical psychologists were then waging. He wrote:

> What in my view characterizes this behavioral psychology in comparison to other branches of psychological study is its constitutional incapacity to grasp and exhibit clearly its own founding project. The founding projects of some of the earlier branches of psychology could at least be seen as running directly counter to

philosophy. But in this case, with any relation whatsoever to philosophical theory being refused at the outset, the question arises of where such a form of psychological research could draw its sense from? By consenting to follow the pattern of biology and become an objective science of aptitudes, reactions, and behavior, this psychology and these psychologists are completely forgetting to situate their specific behavior in relation to historical circumstances, and to the social milieux in which they are led to offer their methods or techniques, and get their services accepted.[56]

Canguilhem's 1956 lecture could be read as a lethal assault on psychology as a discipline aiming to achieve an impossible "unity" and as a warning about the dangers of behavioralism. Ten years later, though, it became a weapon in a new war for which its author had not originally destined it. Nevertheless, when the editors of the journal *Les Cahiers pour l'Analyse*, published by the epistemology circle of the ENS, asked to republish it, he gave them his permission.[57]

At this time, under the influence of Louis Althusser, the students of the rue d'Ulm were strong adherents both of a new reading of the oeuvre of Marx and a return to the oeuvre of Freud on the basis of Lacan's teaching.[58] The task at this point, as far as they were concerned, was to create a theoretical front against spiritual idealism and putatively scientific ideologies, and to set against them a *true science* of revolution based on a triple alliance of Saussurean linguistics, Althusserian Marxism, and Lacanian Freudianism. From this perspective, psychology in all of its ramifications was regarded as a false science in the service of an ideology of servitude and incarceration. And so Canguilhem's 1956 lecture could be seen in a new light as the most ferocious analysis ever produced against the essence of disciplinary power, worthy to be ranked with Foucault's critique of psychiatry.[59]

Canguilhem certainly never shared directly in the ardor of the Althusser-Lacan generation of the rue d'Ulm, as he told me himself more than once. Yet this revolt against psychology, and more precisely against its most instrumentalist branch, behavioralism, did not displease him. He had conceived his lecture as a polemical assault in the first place, and now he had the satisfaction—he who was neither a Marxist nor a Lacanian—of seeing his message bear fruit. For despite the differences between the original text of 1956 and the one presented to the public in 1966, there was indeed a continuity of approach between them: They both advanced a conception of the history of science radically opposed to any reduction of the human to evaluative or mechanistic interpretations of any sort. And it must be added that the man who had refused, in June 1940, to serve Marshal Pétain was not insensible to a certain idea of revolutionary heroism of the kind that marked this whole younger generation, even if he himself never thought for a moment that it was desirable to elaborate any sort of "science" of history, or of subjectivity, on the model of dialectical materialism or the logic of the signifier.

Canguilhem was always hostile to dogmatism and group-think. And he saw too clearly the impasses to which Althusserian Marxism in combination with Lacanian logicism was leading not to adopt a certain reserve vis-à-vis those who nevertheless were citing his own thought.[60] This did not keep him from being a great reader of Freud's work, quite the contrary; nor did it keep him from grasping, like Sartre at the same period,[61] how thoroughly Freud the man was a scientist who conformed to his own outlook on the history of science: a scientist divided between error and truth, a scientist capable of constructing a rational method that was not a science, the object of which could never be encompassed by the discourse of science.

On this point, we might wonder why Canguilhem never devoted even a short article to Freud or to psychoanalysis. No doubt he preferred to address this topic allusively, the better to distance himself from the jargon of the psychoanalytic schools. Perhaps he thought that as it spread, Freudian discourse had come to resemble psychology in its pretensions to scientific status, in its ambition to dictate terms to the other domains of knowledge.

Be that as it may, Canguilhem never softened his stance toward the so-called science of behaviors and assessments. And in 1980, in the great amphitheater of the Sorbonne before an audience of thousands of enthusiastic listeners,[62] that he gave a lecture on the brain and thought in which, adopting a strategy of defending Freud's discoveries in veiled terms, he revived the combat of 1956.[63] Paying homage to Foucault, he was not content now to designate psychology as a philosophy without rigor, an ethics without exigency, and a medicine without control: he portrayed it as a barbarity of the modern age, which had become all the more formidable in that it was now claiming to rely on biology and technical progress in cerebral imaging in order to portray thought as no more than a secretion of the brain.

Though without uttering the word "cognitivism,"[64] which only came into widespread use in France in 1981, Canguilhem attacked the belief underlying the cognitive ideal: the pretension to found a science of the spirit on the idea that mental states can be correlated with brain states. With jubilation he denounced all those who, from Piaget to Chomsky, had dreamed of making thought an empty space, to the point of imagining that a machine might be capable of writing *À la recherche du temps perdu*: "I will gladly refrain from addressing a question that logically ought to lead us to wonder about the possibility of one day seeing, in a bookshop window, *The Autobiography of a Computer*, if not its *Autocritique*."[65]

If the attack was just as blunt as in 1956, it was much more political this time, focusing exclusively on psychology's power of technological oppression. In other words, far from picking a quarrel with clinical psychologists—that is, with the heirs of Daniel Lagache, whose malaise he clearly perceived—Canguilhem directed his fire not at psychology in general but at the branch of it with the pretension to arrive at pure organogenesis by means of a science of the spirit. And he then appealed to Janet, the better to defend Freud.

Citing a text by the French psychologist on the need to keep psychology, as a human science, from being subsumed into a mythology of the brain, he noted that the antipsychiatrists were not wrong to emphasize the shortcomings of a psychopharmacology that thought it could eradicate madness by acting exclusively on the brain. Only Freud, he added, had been able to free himself from illusory typologies and localizations, and thus give meaning to a topographic model of the psyche.

And taking a stance even more radical than he had done in the past, Canguilhem resolutely warned future generations about "the permanent calamity" of a psychology that was now attempting to increase the output of the thinking process without worrying about the meaning of its power. Recalling that, after the assassination of Johan de Witt,[66] Spinoza had left the shelter of his lodgings in order to denounce the perpetrators as *ultimi barbarorum*, the Canguilhem of the 1980s called upon his audience to remember the Canguilhem of June 1940 and the heroic death of Cavaillès. He thus donned the mantle of the founder of a philosophy without the subject, sounding a summons to all men of good will, in the name of the unity of philosophy, in which Cartesians and Spinozists would be united—that is, partisans and adversaries of the philosophy of consciousness, or partisans and adversaries of the philosophy of concepts and the philosophy of commitment—against what might well be called the most liberticide branch of psychology: "At first glance, one might think that Spinoza made a mistake, the mistake of thinking that the barbarians whom he denounced publicly were the last. But he knew Latin, and his meaning was: the most recent, the latest to appear. Thus philosophers of today, whatever their line of research, Spinozist or Cartesian, can be certain that they will not lack occasions or reasons to go out, at their own risk, in a gesture of commitment controlled by their brains, and write on walls, ramparts, or fences: *ultimi barbarorum*."[67]

Knowing that the current exponents of this barbarity are now invoking biological, neuronal, or cerebral reasons to "explain" the supposedly innate differences between the sexes and the races, thus reinventing discriminations we had thought were gone for good, we can only conclude that Canguilhem's injunctions are more than ever worth heeding.[68] Actually, there is nothing more modern than this philosophy of heroism, which was able to unite, at the same time and in a single movement, the loftiest conceptual thought with the most robust political commitment.

Georges Canguilhem disliked talking about either his period as a follower of Alain, his time in the Resistance, or himself, but he always praised the combat of those who reminded him of the spirit of the Resistance. When in 1988 I proposed, as others had already done, writing a book about his career, using the account he had published of Cavaillès as a model, he wrote back as follows: "I continue to think that it is not up to me to comment on what I may have said, written, or done. I continue to think that certain of my old comrades, whose memory I still cherish, might have done better at times not to 'present' themselves, and to let their works alone do the talking. I dislike 'colloquies in honor of' and television interviews. I dislike it when people act as their own expounders."[69]

2. JEAN-PAUL SARTRE

{PSYCHOANALYSIS ON THE SHADOWY BANKS OF THE DANUBE}

O N THE EVE OF WORLD WAR TWO, JEAN-PAUL SARTRE HAD
already published *Nausea*, one of the major novels of the twentieth century. In it he narrates the subjective epic of an individual, one
Antoine Roquentin, whose profound melancholy is linked to the melancholy of a world in disintegration.

Having resided in Berlin and witnessed the triumph of Nazism, Sartre
apparently wanted to express metaphysical truths he had derived from
his reading of the great phenomenological texts of the period, from
Husserl to Heidegger, in the form of an excursion into self-analysis by
a narrator who is adrift. In the course of his confrontation with the notion that "death must justify the living," Roquentin comes to see that the
nausea gripping him is nothing other than existence itself, an existence
without anteriority or essence. He then forgets his past, bit by bit, and
sinks into a present stripped of meaning and composed of "ferocious
respectable folk," the effect of whose ritualized gestures is to push him
to the brink of complete collapse, all the more absurd in that it bears no
relation to any causality.[1]

In 1937, when this novel was already written but not yet published, Sartre feared he would never attain glory. He wrote later: "At thirty-two years of age I felt as old as the world. How remote was the life of a great man I had promised myself. On top of that, I was not very satisfied with what I was writing, and yet would have been delighted to be in print. Today I can gauge the depth of my disappointment when I recall that at age twenty-two I had written this sentence of Töppfer, which caused my heart to beat faster, in my notebook: 'He who is not famous at twenty-eight years of age must renounce glory for ever.'"[2] Yet by the time the war broke out Sartre had become a writer, not a famous one, but at any rate the bearer of a great literary career to come. At one time he had thought that the notion of progress was nonsense. Unlike Canguilhem he had evolved toward a sort of integral pacifism that blinded him to the political importance of Munich: "I was caught between defenders and opponents of the pact of Munich, and here I must confess that I never had the intellectual courage to be one or the other. The pro-Munich crowd disgusted me because they were all bourgeois and cowardly, fearful for their own skins, their capital, or their capitalism. But the anti-Munich crowd seemed scary to me because they wanted a war."[3]

Like Roquentin, Sartre was unreceptive to any form of real commitment in those years, so no heroic philosophy could have attracted him, given that the only acceptable attitude lay in not being with one side or the other, neither with the cowards nor with the combatants. Likewise he fatalistically accepted being called up for military service and held in a prison camp. It was only after the experience of prison life that he began to realize the necessity for commitment. Yet he never made the decisive act so well described by Canguilhem in writing about Cavaillès, the moment of choice in which an intellectual shows himself capable of dying for freedom, even at the cost of his own future oeuvre.

Sartre certainly realized, from the time he returned to Paris, that neutrality was no longer possible. That is why, during the summer of 1941, he, Simone de Beauvoir, and a few others constituted the group Socialism and Liberty with the aim of resisting Vichy, but its existence was fleeting. The fact is that throughout the entire occupation Sartre just went on writing and publishing, though he did maintain contact with writers of the Resistance, notably those grouped around *Lettres Françaises*, who were working in secret.

It was precisely the dialectic between liberty and servitude, as he lived it throughout the period of the war, that converted Sartre to a philosophy of commitment. Simone de Beauvoir's discovery of the female identity took place against the same background: "That it made a difference whether one was Jew or Aryan was something I already knew; but I had never noticed that there was a female condition. Suddenly I encountered a large number of women who were over forty, and who, despite the hazards of luck and merit, had all gone through the same experience: they had lived as *relative beings*."[4]

Similarly, it was through becoming aware of his situation as a captive subject—or relative being—that Sartre evolved, during the occupation and through a range of writings, including *Being and Nothingness*, from a pacifism that he was beginning to challenge toward a true commitment, which took concrete form only after the war. His conversion to a philosophy of freedom occurred with the publication of a celebrated article, "The Republic of Silence," which includes these paradoxical words:

> Never were we more free than under the German occupation. We had lost our rights, starting with the right to speak: they insulted us to our faces every day and we had to keep silent; they deported us en masse, as workers, as Jews, as political prisoners; everywhere, on walls, in newspapers, on the screen, we kept seeing the dirty and dull visage our oppressors wanted to give us of ourselves: because of all that we were free. . . . Thus the very question of freedom was posed, and we were on the brink of the most profound knowledge man can have of himself. For the secret of man is not his Oedipus complex, or inferiority complex, it is the very limit of his liberty, it is his power of resistance to torture and death.[5]

In paying homage to all those who had been genuine resisters (unlike himself), Sartre attacks a certain psychologization of man caused by the overused notion of the Oedipus complex; Canguilhem was to do the same thing in his own way. The act of resistance, Sartre says in substance, always relates to a radical stripping bare of the human condition, and it is on that basis—from out of exile, cruelty, torture, the unbearable—that every subject can gauge himself against a universal of liberty that requires no psychological "explanation." In other words, the choice of a heroic death does not depend on any conscious decision but rather on a confrontation with the horror of a possible annihilation of the self.

One understands how this testament to the glory of those who had died caused Sartre to be seen as a pioneering figure of the anti-Nazi Resistance by the generations who made their mark in the second half of the twentieth century, though Sartre himself had been unable or unwilling to die for freedom. No imposture was at work! Sometimes words are so close to deeds that they catalyze the collective desire. From that perspective, the Sartrean "we" of 9 September 1944 overlaps with the famous words with which Charles de Gaulle put an end to the national humiliation on 25 August 1944: "Paris! Paris offended! Paris broken! Paris martyrized! But Paris liberated, liberated by itself, liberated by its people with the aid of the armies of France, with the support and aid of the whole of France, of the France that is fighting, of the only France."[6]

Sartre and de Gaulle, whose destinies were interwoven throughout the second half of the century, incarnate the values inhering in the spirit of resistance, each in his own way. The combat that Sartre had not waged between 1940 and 1944 he did wage during the Algerian war, when he took the side of those who were struggling against colonialism. After de Gaulle had ended that war, Sartre took sides against him during the student revolt of May 1968 and contributed to his political defeat.

However, if Sartre was able to convert to the cause of freedom, that is because, during the darkest hours of the occupation, he had faced up to writing the 729 pages of *Being and Nothingness*.[7] When this work appeared, daily life in defeated France was devoted to waiting and was sunk in ennui. It was divided between the hustle of the black market and the humiliation of living in the aftermath of total disaster. Only the handful of men whom Sartre would celebrate in September 1944 had retained the taste for freedom. But for the moment this combat had no other horizon than the certitude of approaching death. At Caluire the enemy had struck at the soul of the Resistance. Handed over to the Gestapo, tortured and killed, Jean Moulin had not had time to fulfill his mission to unify the leaders of the clandestine struggle. Yet on the fields of battle, victory was in the offing. In the south, the allies were approaching the coast of Sicily, and in the north the Red Army was preparing its grand offensive.

In this context, the great philosophical edifice erected by Sartre and inspired by German phenomenology revealed how much the world at war was thirsting for liberty. And if liberty remained, in Sartrean terms, the stake in the battle between the opposing forces of alienation and existential intentionality, that was because it escaped pure mastery, because no subject was capable of choosing it in full responsibility. Liberty might be the finest flower of consciousness; that did not prevent consciousness from being riddled with mental processes authorizing the subject to shelter behind the deceptive screen of constant "bad faith."

Sartre here expressed for the first time his philosophical position with regard to the Freudian unconscious, and he revealed what his reference texts were. It was evident that he had read the principal works of Freud translated into French between 1920 and 1940.[8] Hence he possessed a wide acquaintance with the domains of dreaming, sexuality, transference, the impulses, repression, Freudian slips, and the Oedipus complex.

It is well known that Freud's concept of the unconscious relied on two successive theories of psychical organization. The first, constructed at the beginning of the century, comprises three systems: the unconscious, the site of censure and repression; the preconscious; and the conscious. The last two systems form an organization called the general system of consciousness, which gives an incomplete view of human processes. The second theory, advanced in 1920, overlays the first, which it corrects by accentuating the primacy of the unconscious. It comprises the id, the center of the impulses; the ego, the site of representations; and the superego, which plays the role of judge with regard to the ego.

It is the ensemble formed by these two topographies that Sartre comments upon in part 1, chapter 2 of *Being and Nothingness*, without seeking to understand how Freud's conception had undergone modification over an interval of twenty years. Sartre did not concern himself with questions of this kind because, in his eyes, the Freudian unconscious was a useless concept, too mechanistic and too biological in any case for thinking the secret intentionality that governs all human existence. So it was better to replace it with the notion of "bad faith," which, integrated into the notion of consciousness, allowed him to define a sort of pathology of ambivalence, in which the subject is condemned to unite, in a single act, an idea and the negation of that idea, a transcendence and a facticity. In the same perspective, Sartre refused so-called empirical psychoanalysis—that of Freud himself—and preferred what he called "existential" psychoanalysis. He accused empirical psychoanalysis of denying dialectic and of failing to recognize the essence of freedom because of its emphasis on the initial affectivity of the individual (who thus becomes "virgin wax prior to history"). He saw existential psychoanalysis as having the capacity to abolish the unconscious and affirm that nothing exists prior to the original welling up of freedom.

Note that Sartre did not appeal to the usual figures of French anti-Freudianism in opposing the Freudian project. He did not liken the theory of sexuality to a pansexualism of German origin; he did not think the unconscious under the category of a subconscious in the manner of Pierre Janet; and finally he did not claim that psychoanalysis was incompatible with a Cartesianism putatively rational and "French" as opposed to being obscurantist and "German." Actually he did not in the strict sense reject the Freudian unconscious, but he did subject it to a sort of doctrinal torsion for the purpose of showing that the mental processes that escape the consciousness of the subject do belong to the domain of the conscious—provided that it was conceived in phenomenological terms.[9] Since Sartre made consciousness an intentionality, and man a project whose existence precedes its essence, it was possible for him to replace the topographic system, in which the unconscious predominates, with a transcendental system in which the phenomenon of the unconscious became in effect a latent consciousness. Hence the Freudian concept of the unconscious lost its usefulness, although the figures of repression and misrecognition were preserved in the register of consciousness.

Eugène Minkowski had tried before Sartre, but without success from the point of view of psychiatric knowledge, to forge a link between Freudian discourse and phenomenology. Lacan had subsequently been tempted by the same perspective. But from 1936 on, despite making considerable use of the phenomenological vocabulary, Lacan had chosen a different course, on account of the privileged place he accorded to the Freudian unconscious. This is why Sartre in 1943 was the first French theorist to propose a truly phenomenological reading of the Freudian unconscious. It is no surprise that he integrated it into a philosophy of human liberty, for as Michel Foucault showed, from 1929 on, two interpretations of Husserlian phenomenology were possible. One looked toward a philosophy of the subject (Sartre and Merleau-Ponty), while the other aimed at renewing a philosophy of concepts, of knowledge, and the history of science (Koyré, Canguilhem, and Cavaillès).[10] Lacan's position between these two filiations would remain paradoxical: in his nonphenomenological reformulation of the unconscious he showed that he was choosing the second, but his constant interrogation of the status of the subject shows that he did not break cleanly with the first (through it, in fact, his discourse intersected with Sartre's).

Right after World War Two the discovery of Marxism transformed Sartre's views on psychoanalysis, though without modifying his position on the uselessness of the Freudian unconscious. The philosopher then sought in the Viennese doctrine a method of understanding the individual in all his facets. He thus became a Freudo-Marxist, in the sense that he attempted to connect the two doctrines of emancipation—to change the subject, to change society—in order to interpret the historico-subjective meaning of human destinies. It was in a screenplay entitled *L'engrenage* that he explained his new project for the first time: "to figure out how the private and the public combine in the case of a statesman. . . . By combining Marxist and psychoanalytic analyses, it ought to be possible to show how a certain society and a certain childhood form someone who will be capable of taking and exercising power in the name of his group."[11]

When Sartre was writing this screenplay, the international psychoanalytic movement was bearing the full brunt of the partition of Yalta. In the United States, thanks to the great waves of immigration, Freud's teaching was expanding rapidly, but at the cost of blending into hygienist ideals foreign to its origins. In the Soviet Union, on the other hand, it was the target of a violent attack, even though its last practitioners there had vanished in 1930, and no new psychoanalytic movement had come into being.[12] Soviet anti-Freudianism in the 1950s was a form of anti-Americanism. It was focused less on critiquing Freud's theories as such, as in the 1930s, than on combating what was customarily called "American psychoanalysis," meaning the kind of adaptive neo-Freudianism characteristic of psychoanalysis in the American setting, which the communists branded "a reactionary ideology in the service of American imperialism."[13]

The anti-Freudian campaign conducted by the communists was rendered more virulent still by the attitude of the international psychiatric-psychoanalytic movement, which was attempting, through the World Health Organization, to promote the idea that the great dictatorships reflected the personal madness of their protagonists. In this psychologized interpretation of political phenomena, the origins of Nazism and Stalinism lay in Hitler's hysteria and Stalin's paranoia. At the Third International Congress on Mental Hygiene in London in 1948, some practitioners even went so far as to propose that statesmen be given treatment in order to reduce their aggressive instincts and preserve world peace.

Evidently the rapprochement effected by Sartre between Marxism and psychoanalysis was not unconnected to this polemic. But rather than playing the bipolar game of combating psychoanalysis in the name of the communist ideal and communism in the name of the "sound health" of heads of state, the philosopher preferred to bring the critical function of the Freudo-Marxism of the 1930s up to date by making it face the questions posed by the contemporary world.

Nine years later in *Questions of Method* he gave philosophic content to his Freudo-Marxism.[14] Existentialism was then conceived by Sartre as a philosophy interpreting human actions and human creativity. Consequently the solution to human destiny had to follow from a systematic exploration of infancy. Yet while asserting the need for a return to the origins, Sartre stigmatized psychobiography:

Today only psychoanalysis allows us to study in depth the process by which a child, feeling its way in the dark, tries to play, though it doesn't understand, the social role that adults impose on it. . . . Psychoanalysis alone permits us to rediscover the whole man inside the adult, meaning not just his present determining factors, but also the weight of his history. And it would be quite mistaken to imagine that this discipline is opposed to dialectical materialism. Of course some amateurs in the West have constructed "analytic" theories about society and history which spill over in effect into idealism. How many times have we been served up the psychoanalysis of Robespierre? . . . In fact, dialectical materialism can no longer do without the privileged mediation that allows it to move from general and abstract determining factors to certain traits of the particular individual. Psychoanalysis has no principles, it has no theoretical basis: at most it is accompanied—in Jung and in some of Freud's works—by a perfectly inoffensive mythology.[15]

Thus Sartre's second reading of Freud followed on the one introduced in *Being and Nothingness*. But the philosopher was now employing Marxism as the critical weapon for his rejection of the empirical and "unprincipled" character of psychoanalysis.

But through this seemingly rigorous Freudo-Marxist approach, Sartre's aim was always to define a subjectivity capable of uncovering its own thought and identity in those of another. Hence the Sartrean method, existential or Freudo-Marxist, was no longer adequate to the object it claimed to interpret. In reality it functioned at one moment as a doctrinal superego, through which Sartre sought authorization from psychoanalysis to deny Freudianism the essence of its own discovery, and at another as a *Bildung* that might allow him to tame the real object of his interpretation.

In this respect, the conflictual relation that Sartre always maintained vis-à-vis psychoanalysis and the figure of Freud is of the same order as the relation that he ended by establishing with Flaubert. You could even say that it was in order to know the writer who had dared to say "Madame Bovary c'est moi" that Sartre, from the time of *Being and Nothingness*, had dreamed of inventing a psychoanalysis capable of explaining the situation, both free and signifying, of the exceptional man.

Hence this existential psychoanalysis would be centered not on Freudian slips, neuroses, and dreams, but on accomplishments of style and thought. In sum, Sartre went so far as to imagine a possible psychoanalysis of the consciousness of self, with himself as its founding father: "This psychoanalysis has not yet found its Freud: at most we can detect the presentiment of it in certain particularly successful biographies. It is my hope to be able to supply two examples elsewhere, in connection with Flaubert and Dostoyevsky. But here it matters little for me whether or not it exists; the important thing for me is that it be possible."[16]

The Freud/Flaubert symmetry functions perfectly here. Sartre basically announces that he will not succeed in writing his great work on Flaubert until he has become the Freud of a psychoanalysis that has jettisoned the unconscious. To put it another way, the composition of his work on Flaubert remains dependent, as far as he is concerned, on the invention of a method that will allow it to be composed. And the latter, so Sartre believed, he would be able to perfect following the war, by bringing Freudo-Marxism up to date. But the idea soon occurred to him of trying it out on himself, and he decided to write his autobiography: "I would like to avoid the novelistic approach, and even omit circumstantial details where they lack importance. These will be memoirs in which I shall define myself in relation to the historical situation, employing a version of psychoanalysis and the Marxist method as systems of investigation. It matters greatly to me to explain the reason for which I write. . . . I would like in this work to explain almost everything about myself, why it happens that I still wish to write according to a certain form of aesthetic, but have come to participate in social events: how I burst forth."[17]

This research occupied Sartre for ten years. But between April and September 1957 he simultaneously began the writing of his great work on Flaubert and gave a Freudo-Marxist content to his existential philosophy. The appearance of *Questions of Method*,[18] which served as a preface to his *Critique of Dialectical Reason*, coincided in effect with that of the earliest articles that were to become *The Idiot of the Family*.[19] At this date Sartre seemed to have achieved the aspiration proclaimed in *Being and Nothingness*: to become the Freud of a psychoanalysis without the unconscious, fit at last to grasp man in his totality.

To put it another way, he declares allegiance to a Freudianism of "bad faith" in order to initiate himself into a new interpretive method. But this double relation to a doctrinal superego and a *Bildung* allowed him neither to complete his autobiography nor to devote himself wholeheartedly to completing his study of Flaubert. It would seem that the intellectual toolkit he had assembled following *Being and Nothingness* did nothing but sterilize Sartre's writing, and that it had to be made to implode so that the recital of himself and the biography of Flaubert could both "burst forth."

It was the film director John Huston who in 1958 gave Sartre the chance to break out of his own system. When Huston commissioned Sartre to write a screenplay on the life and work of Sigmund Freud, elements of psychoanalysis had already found their way into the movies. But Hollywood's psychoanalysis was not that of the psychoanalytic community in the United States, even though, as emigrants from old Europe, many American film directors had a shared background with the psychoanalysts who were members of the International Psychoanalytical Association.[20]

Exile had not, however, had the same effect on the two groups. Whereas the therapists had chosen to integrate into the American health system (which obliged them to pursue medical careers and become servants of a hygienist ideal[21]), the filmmakers had adopted Freud's doctrine and transformed it into a powerful tool for criticizing the ideals of the American way of life. So it came about that Freudianism was made to serve the interests of an ideal of society on one hand and was used to criticize its adaptive aberrations or to reconnect with the high tradition of European psychoanalysis on the other. Examples of the latter would include Elia Kazan, who drew a daunting portrait of the puritan America of the 1930s in *Splendor in the Grass*, and Charlie Chaplin, who in *Limelight* re-created the London of his childhood in telling the story of an amorous dancer who is cured of her paralysis by a clown with a middle European appearance.[22]

Though he was American born, John Huston shared this dissenting and nostalgic ideal. His purpose in making a biography of Freud was to highlight the original moment of discovery. This is why, wishing to criticize the official psychoanalysis of American psychiatrists, he turned to Sartre, a man of the left and a philosopher of freedom not known for indulging in Freudian hagiography. Transformed into a Sartrean hero, Huston's onscreen Freud thus had the potential to be a true adventurer of modern science, combined with a tragic hero of sorts straight from the pages of *No Exit*.[23]

At the end of 1958 Sartre sent Huston a ninety-five-page synopsis, which led to a firm contract. A few months later he completed a new version, but alas, it was too long to be filmed. Then in October 1959 Sartre traveled with Arlette El Kaïm to Huston's home in Ireland, so they could work together on a final shooting script. The encounter turned into a bout of intellectual pugilistics. Incapable of either mutual understanding or mutual respect, the two men, so alike and yet so different, kept trying to dominate each other, until the final misunderstanding was hatched: a superb but unfilmable screenplay, and a fascinating failure of a film.[24]

Huston saw Sartre as a man completely unable to listen to anyone else, for whom the body did not exist:

> He made notes—of his own words—as he talked. There was no such thing as a conversation with him; he talked incessantly, and there was no interrupting him. You'd wait for him to catch his breath, but he wouldn't. The words came out in an absolute torrent. . . . Sartre was a little barrel of a man, and as ugly as a human being can be. His face was both bloated and pitted, his teeth were yellowed and he was wall-eyed. He wore a gray suit, black shoes, white shirt, tie and vest. His appearance never changed. He'd come down in the morning in this suit, and he would still be wearing it the last thing at night. The suit always appeared to be clean, and his shirt was clean, but I never knew if he owned one gray suit or several identical gray suits. . . . One morning he came down and his cheek was swollen. He had a bad tooth. I said, "We'd best get you to Dublin with that." "No, no. Let's just go in to Galway." I didn't know any dentist in Galway, but that didn't matter to him. So we made an appointment with a local dentist and took him in.

He was out in a few minutes, having had the tooth pulled. A tooth more or less made no difference in Sartre's cosmos. The physical world he left to others; his was of the mind.[25]

As for Sartre, the gaze he cast on Huston's world in his letters to Simone de Beauvoir was the ferocious one of a body snatcher:

Through a number of similar rooms wanders a tall romantic, sad and isolated: our friend Huston, perfectly vacant, literally incapable of speaking to those whom he has invited. . . . What a lot of babble there is here! Everyone has his own complex, ranging from masochism to animal fierceness. Don't imagine, though, that we are in hell. It's more like an enormous cemetery, full of corpses with their frozen complexes. . . . The inner landscape of my boss, the great Huston, is a lot like that: heaps of ruins, abandoned houses, plots of wasteland, swamps, a thousand traces of human presence. But the man himself has emigrated, I have no idea where. He isn't even gloomy: he is empty, except in his moments of infantile vanity when he dons a red tuxedo, or goes horseback riding (not very well), or reviews his paintings and directs his workers. It is impossible to hold his attention for five minutes: he has lost the capacity for work, and he avoids reasoning.[26]

Nevertheless, Sartre and Huston were thinking along the same lines about what to feature in the life of Freud. Both wished to illustrate the groundbreaking moment when a scientist takes the step that will make him the founder of a new science. In Freud's case this was the moment when he gave hysteria the status of a true neurosis by reintroducing into its etiology the question of sexuality, which Charcot had blanked out and detached from simulation, in order to make hysteria a functional illness. The foregrounding of sexual etiology guided Freud toward the discovery of an unconscious independent of consciousness and nonpsychological in nature, down a path opened up by the interpretation of dreams and the elaboration of the notions of fantasy and transference. This feat was not accomplished at one stroke, and Freud's advance toward the truth was continuously disturbed by the shadows of error. As Sartre said: "To arrive at correct ideas, you have to begin by explaining false ideas, and that is a long process. . . . Which we tried to do—and that's what interested Huston above all, not when Freud's theories had already made him famous but the time when, at around age thirty, he had got things completely wrong and his ideas had led him to a desperate impasse."[27]

To flesh out his protagonist, Sartre put to work all the knowledge of psychoanalytic culture that he had acquired since writing *Being and Nothingness*. But he also added three new sources previously unknown to him: the letters of Freud to Wilhelm Fliess, published in French in 1956 under the title *La naissance de la psychanalyse*, the *Studies on Hysteria* that appeared in the same year (comprising Josef Breuer's account of the case of Anna O.), and finally the first volume in English of the monumental Freud biography by Ernest Jones, from which Michèle Vian had read him a number of chapters while she was working on the French translation.[28] Through these works he became acquainted with Freud's complex relationships with three of the major figures in his intellectual formation: Theodor Meynert, Breuer, and Fliess. He also discovered two versions of the story of Anna O., Breuer's and especially Jones's, which assigned this female hysteric a role that became legendary in the history of the psychoanalytic movement.[29] Additionally there was the episode of Freud's meeting with Martin Charcot at la Salpêtrière.

Sartre condensed into a unified drama events that had actually unfolded between 1885 and 1908, which I briefly summarize. Basing himself on Charcot's theses, Freud had tried to demonstrate the existence of masculine hysteria to his Viennese colleagues. The point at issue was fundamental, because if it were once established that hysteria were a psychical illness unrelated to the uterus and thus to the genital organs, it would apply as much to men as it did to women, even though the symptoms might be expressed most severely in women. In order to detach hysteria from its genital substratum, Charcot moved away from a sexual etiology. In Vienna, Freud clashed especially with the redoubtable Meynert, his instructor in psychiatry, who in denying the existence of masculine hysteria was actually rejecting the modern conception of hysteria advanced by Charcot.[30]

In this great epic of genesis, in which Freud advanced toward a new conception of the unconscious, such conflicts amounted to more than mere abstract jousts. The opponents were men of flesh and blood, themselves suffering from the very symptoms whose existence they were debating. Meynert, an eccentric character, a liar, an alcoholic, and a neurotic, understood perfectly well what was at stake, even though he did not grasp its importance for the history of science. A good clinician, he knew that his own case was one of hysteria, and that therefore hysteria might very well occur in males. The struggle he waged against Freud over a matter of science was none the less neurotic or subjective for that. Before dying he confessed the nature of his "illness" to Freud and revealed his art of dissimulation to him.[31]

That Charcot had been forced to set aside the genital substratum in order to give a new definition of hysteria did not prevent the scientists of the late nineteenth century from accepting the importance of the sexual factor in the genesis of the neuroses. But none of them was able to *theorize* this hypothesis, which went back to antiquity. Freud alone proved capable of breaking through this barrier by shifting the *whole* problematic away from the terrain of genitality. In the initial phase, it was the interest he took in the case of a young woman of the Vienna bourgeoisie, Bertha Pappenheim, whom Breuer was treating using the "cathartic" method, that enabled Freud to locate the sexual origin of neurosis. He subsequently extended this diagnosis to other cases of female hysteria, while Breuer remained aloof. In the second phase, an even more audacious gesture was required, since Freud had to turn away from the spectacle of what could be observed, and imagine a reality all the more true in that it lay concealed behind the appearances of a deceptive evidentness.

Freud accomplished this gesture while in contact with the Berlin physician Wilhelm Fliess, between 1892 and 1902. Throughout their relationship, which he would later refer to as his *self-analysis*, he was continuously in error. And not content to propose and then refute erroneous hypotheses, he and Fliess traded patients who served as guinea pigs in Freud's chaotic advance toward the truth.[32]

Reversing the position of Charcot, he accepted the evidence of sexual causality in the origin of the neuroses. Certain subjects, he said, undergo real traumas in childhood or during the course of their lives. In the street or in the family setting, children are often seduced, raped, or sexually exploited by adults and relatives. The memory of these traumas is so painful that they prefer to forget or repress them. Hearing such stories recounted by Viennese women, Freud came to accept the validity of what they were saying, and constructed his first hypothesis concerning repression upon the so-called seduction theory. He thought that, because they really had been seduced, hysterical women were afflicted with neurotic disturbances. He then proceeded to accuse fathers all over the world, including his own, of being perverts.

Fliess did not push him in this direction, but tried to make Freud accept a conception of science in which error and experiment would have no place, with totalitarian certitude overriding genuine speculation. An adept of a theory of sexuality both mystical and organicist, Fliess related nasal mucous to genital activity,[33] thought that life was conditioned by periodic phenomena related to the bisexual nature of the human construct, and had already noted the polymorphous character of infantile sexuality. Falling entirely under the spell of Fliess's paranoiac seduction, Freud abandoned his own false seduction theory and evolved toward a conception of science capable of accounting for the reality confronting him.[34]

By dint of listening to hysterical patients, Freud came up against an impossibility: not all fathers are rapists, and yet hysterics are not lying when they say they are victims of sexual seduction on their part. He was therefore compelled to advance a hypothesis that could account for two contradictory verities. Freud accomplished this by retreating from hard evidence. He perceived two things: on one hand women invent, without lying or feigning, seduction scenes that never took place, and on the other, even if these seductions have taken place, they do not explain the outbreak of a neurosis. To explain these two facts and make them consistent, Freud replaced the seduction theory with the theory of sexual fantasy, opening the road to a doctrine of psychical reality grounded in the unconscious.

It is well known that all Freud's contemporaries had conceived of the existence of this famous "other scene," but there is no doubt that he was the first to indicate its function in resolving the enigma of sexual causation: sexual causation originates in fantasy, even when a real trauma has occurred, because the reality of fantasy is of a different kind than material reality. In taking this step, Freud freed himself from Fliess's seduction, though Fliess himself had never been a follower of the seduction theory.

In 1958 the sources available to Sartre were incomplete. Not only had the correspondence with Fliess been expurgated by Freud's heirs, to the point that it failed to convey the terrible mistakes into which Freud had been drawn, but Jones's account of the history of Bertha Pappenheim did not conform in the least to the historical truth.[35] Yet notwithstanding these deficiencies, Sartre's Freud was both truer than life and less fictional than the Freud, part authoritarian and part tranquil paterfamilias, portrayed in the pages of Ernest Jones. Instead of riveting his hero to a putatively linear destiny, in the manner of psychobiography, Sartre pulled off the tour de force of portraying a Faustian scientist, a creature of light and shadow, haunted by desire and sexuality and in revolt against the established order. It is impossible not to be reminded of Bertolt Brecht's Galileo in the theater and Alexandre Koyre's Galileo in the history of science.[36]

Sartre was well aware of the unwontedness of his own position. He who had always denied the existence of the unconscious was now dealing at close quarters with its inventor—a Sartrean situation par excellence, so brilliantly did it illustrate the idea that one discovers in the other, and *against* the other, what one is oneself. Sartre's Freud was thus the contrary of Sartre: a paterfamilias of bourgeois lifestyle, he never had a woman other than his wife after marriage. Doubtless this was because sexual probity was a necessary condition of his advance toward a new definition of human sexuality. If Freud had had carnal relations with the hysterics who offered themselves to his gaze, he would have been unable either to theorize transference or understand the erroneous character of the seduction theory. Such was his destiny as a man of science.

Sartre accepted these evident facts. But he could not help attributing a Sartrean approach to the founding father. Freud, he said, "is a man who undertakes to know others because he sees it as the only way to know himself, and he sees that he must conduct his research on others and on himself. One knows oneself through others, one knows others through oneself."[37] A curious dialectical reversal, since in fact we know that Freud proceeded in exactly the opposite way. Not succeeding in knowing others, he had been forced to discover himself in order to find out about others. That the real Freud had not been "philosophically" Sartrean did not prevent Sartre from reconstructing a perfectly Freudian Freud: more rigorous, for that matter, and truer than the one Freud himself wished to portray in his *Selbstdarstellung*.[38] For Sartre had at his disposal an instrument not available to Freud: a theory of the subject grounded in a philosophy of consciousness. That alone was capable of making this character exist as he journeyed from error toward truth along the twisting path of a ruse of the intellect.

As his counterpart, Sartre invented an astonishing Fliess, a sort of interwar Mephisto right out of the world of Thomas Mann. A doppelganger of Freud, a visionary like him, devilishly Nietzschean, he seems to belong to that race of scientists doomed to failure, who prefer making bargains with the dark powers to giving up their false hypotheses. As molded by Sartre, Fliess thus becomes Freud's Mister Hyde, his impulsive archangel, his bad conscience. Here the philosopher readily plays on the opposition between the two antagonistic sites of Germanic culture: on one hand Vienna, the soft, carefree, vain, anti-Semitic city, and on the other the liberal city of Berlin, open to the Enlightenment and to progress. Each is here portrayed as jealous of the other, just as Freud was jealous of Fliess and vice versa. Filled with Prussian arrogance, the Sartrean Fliess has all the features of an ultraleftist of genitality, a sort of Wilhelm Reich before the fact, who pushes Freud to accept the false theory of seduction so as to avoid having to revise his own conceptions of sexuality. One is reminded of the von Gerlach family in *The Condemned of Altona*, a work for the stage written in the same period as the *Freud* screenplay.[39] A believer in hygienism, Fliess is fundamentally presented by Sartre as a figure of the superego, disparaging Vienna and its disorder, and continually attempting to keep Freud from indulging in his favorite vice: tobacco.

As for Meynert, he appears as the living incarnation of the theory of bad faith Sartre had put forward in *Being and Nothingness*. Crushed for having lied to himself, this celebrated Viennese physician, in his Sartrean incarnation, at once resembles Fliess for extravagance and Breuer for submission to the established order. For the rest, Sartre presents him as a classic case of male hysteria, a character abject one moment and capable of arousing sympathy the next.

In this whole affair among men, in which Freud moved from a powerful revolt against his father to the invention of the Oedipus complex, meaning in Sartrean terms from alienation to liberty, women play an important role. There are the wives and mothers first of all: Amalia, Freud's mother; Martha, his wife; Mathilde, the wife of Breuer. Bourgeois conformists, they are not depicted as ridiculous characters but as vanquished heroines incapable of acceding to freedom. Constrained by conjugal love and maternity, they contribute nothing, according to Sartre, to the intellectual adventure that torments the men whose existence they share. Thus they are both excluded from the realm of creativity and victimized by an inner terror that is no more than the expression of their alienation. At the opposite end of the spectrum, Sartre creates the splendid reign of the hysterical woman Anna O., here rebaptized Cecily.

In the screenplay she is made to bear the extreme unhappiness of the female condition at the end of the nineteenth century. Flesh girded with shame; speech rent with anguish; features reduced to a mouthed howl; incomprehensible movements; frenetic agitations; paralysis; deafness: these are the ravages inscribed on women's bodies by the prohibition of pleasure. But in making a pact with witchery the Sartrean hysteric becomes a free subject, so strongly does her alienation exhibit the world's madness compacted into the solitude of an individual madness. Thus do the wounds of an individual neurosis connect with the universality of the human condition, making the Sartrean subject a hybrid being, half man, half woman, charged with embodying the intermittent figures of desire and revolt. And it is at this limit point that she encounters the great listener, Freud.

Sartre wanted Marilyn Monroe to play Cecily in the movie. She would indeed have been magnificent starring opposite Montgomery Clift as Freud. Huston had already cast them together in *The Misfits*.[40] In some respects the relation between Marilyn Monroe and psychoanalysis could itself have been made into a film focused on what Freudianism became in American society in the 1950s rather than on the nocturnal splendor of its origins. At the same time that John Huston was trying to bring to life a Freud divided between existential doubt and access to the truth, his heirs who had immigrated to the United States had turned into servants of a psychology of normality utterly unconnected to the great Viennese drama reinvented by Sartre.

Marilyn Monroe was first analyzed by Margaret Hohenberg beginning in 1954, at a time when she was using and abusing sedatives and sleeping pills freely provided by various doctors. Three years later Marilyn decided to try a different analyst's couch. She had just married Arthur Miller, who was himself in analysis with the brilliant Rudolph Loewenstein,[41] and she was advised by Anna Freud to enter analysis with Marianne Kris.

Personal history and family genealogy conspired to make Marianne Kris the daughter, so to speak, of psychoanalysis, and the direct heir of the saga of its origins that Huston wanted to film. Her father, Oskar Rie, had been Freud's partner in the game of tarot in Vienna, and her mother was the sister of Ida Bondy, Breuer's former patient and Fliess's wife. Settling first in London and then in New York, Marianne Kris had become the guardian of the official historiography of Freudianism in the 1950s.

There is no doubt that her influence caused Marilyn to refuse to play the role of Cecily, although she said she was delighted to be offered the part by Huston. The fact is that Anna Freud disapproved of the project and had let her friend Kris know as much.[42] Overwhelmed by the difficulty of Marilyn's treatment, and evidently incapable of managing it correctly, Marianne Kris asked Ralph Greenson, who had settled in Santa Monica after his training on the couch of Otto Fenichel, to take charge of Marilyn during his visits to Hollywood. Greenson accepted and immediately sent her to one of his colleagues to receive prescription medicines by injection; nor did he hesitate to give her strong doses of psychoactive drugs of every kind himself. Characterizing her as "borderline, a paranoid drug addict, and a schizophrenic," he tried to convince her to give up the acting profession and her love affairs. Worse, he convinced her to hire as her housekeeper a certain Eunice Murray, a woman with ties to the Jehovah's Witnesses who soon began administering so called substitution treatments to Marilyn.

Drug-dependent and subjected to pressure from various psychoanalysts, themselves in difficulty and terrified at the thought that she might commit suicide, Marilyn drifted into a disastrous state of seclusion that led her to suicide. In August 1962, two months after the tragedy, Anna Freud consoled Greenson, who had sunk into depression: "I am horribly saddened about Marilyn Monroe. I know exactly what you are feeling. . . . One tries and tries in one's head to think how one might have done better, and that leaves a terrible feeling of defeat. But you should know that in these cases I think that we really are defeated by something stronger than we are, compared to which analysis, with all its powers, is too feeble a weapon. When I read in the papers that she had lived with twelve foster families, it made me think of the children in the concentration camps whom we try to treat in our clinic."[43]

Pondering now the impression of strangeness that would have resulted from the onscreen interaction of the two "sacred monsters" of the Hollywood star system, Montgomery Clift and Marilyn Monroe—both haunted by the meanderings of a deadly destiny—one can't help but think that, if the actress's psychoanalysts were unable to forestall her desire for death, they might at least have avoided getting so far lost in the arcana of official history as to be blind to the importance of Huston's project.

As for Sartre, he did not lack boldness, since he dared to situate the scene during which Freud renounced his seduction theory partly in a bordello and partly on a bank of the Danube. In the screenplay, Cecily wanders through Vienna after having made accusations of rape against her father. She goes into a bordello, where Freud comes looking for her in order to take her home in a carriage. It is then that she tells him of the true memory she had repressed since childhood. One day, she relates, she surprised her father embracing her governess and fell downstairs. But when Freud, still believing in the validity of his own theory, shows his incredulity, she threatens to throw herself into the river. Only then does Freud, in a dramatic volte-face, confess his own error to her in turn. Here is the scene:

FREUD: Cecily, you never wanted to slander your father. It was I who forced you to it. You resisted me for as long as you could.
CECILY: Why did you force me?
FREUD: Because I had deceived myself.[44]

The veritable history of this true "scene" of renunciation is found in the correspondence of the real Freud with the real Fliess. It took place in written form, did not occur between a bordello and the Danube, and did not bring in the challenge of the female condition in so direct a manner. Yet the violence of the theoretical gesture, with the avowal made by one man to another in the privacy of written communication, is analogous to the violence of the nocturnal banquet imagined by Sartre, in which the confession is extracted by a woman from a man, who in this way frees her from her fetters by inventing transference.

Here, in the translation of Jeffrey Moussaieff Masson, are some portions of the letter of 21 September 1897—called the "equinox letter"—so often commented upon by historians of Freudianism:[45]

I no longer believe in my *neurotica* [theory of the neuroses]. This is probably not intelligible without an explanation; after all, you yourself found credible what I was able to tell you. So I will begin historically [and tell you] where the reasons for disbelief came from. The continual disappointment in my efforts to bring a single analysis to a real conclusion; the running away of people who for a period of time had been most gripped [by analysis]; the absence of the complete successes on which I had counted; the possibility of explaining to myself the partial successes in other ways, in the usual fashion—this was the first group. Then the surprise that in all cases, the *father*, not excluding my own, had to be accused of being perverse—the realization of the unexpected frequency of hysteria, with precisely the same conditions prevailing in each, whereas surely such widespread perversions against children are not very probable. . . . Then, third, the certain insight that there are no indications of reality in the unconscious, so that one cannot distinguish between truth and fiction that has been cathected with affect. . . . Fourth, the consideration that in the most deep-reaching psychosis the unconscious memory does not break through, so that the secret of childhood experiences is not disclosed even in the most confused delirium. . . . [T]o be cheerful is everything! I could indeed feel quite discontent. The expectation of eternal fame was so beautiful, as was that of certain wealth, complete independence, travels, and lifting the children above the severe worries that robbed me of my youth. Everything depended upon whether or not hysteria would come out right. Now I can once again remain quiet and modest, go on worrying and saving. A little story from my collection occurs to me: "Rebecca, take off your gown; you are no longer a bride."[46]

The version of this letter available to Sartre in 1958 is as incomplete as the account of it given by Jones. For one thing, it omits the passage in which Freud incriminates his father, who had died eleven months previously,[47] and the whole concluding part in which he details, not without humor, the glorious situation that would have been his had his false theory been proven accurate. Now, Sartre reestablishes the truth in an almost excessive fashion. Making wonderful use of chronology—the death of Jakob precedes Freud's abandonment of the seduction theory—he shows that Freud renounced his error too late to have had time to make peace with his father, upon whom the famous suspicion of seduction still weighs. So the only solution remaining for him is a "Freudian" one: posthumous reconciliation with the symbolic figure of paternity, which will lead him to elaborate the idea of the superego.

In other words, in the screenplay Sartre was playing the card of a Freudian Freud against himself, the better to demonstrate that in Sartrean terms the acceptance of such a figure and such a notion is impossible. Doubtless it was because he had invented this Freud, conforming rigorously to the reality of the history of Freudianism, that he freed himself from the doctrinal superego of his own existential Freudo-Marxism, which was hampering his writing, his autobiography, and the completion of his great work on Flaubert.

The Sartrean act of liberation could then be expanded in *The Words*, in the course of a vehement diatribe by the narrator against his father literally marked by Freud's action in renouncing the seduction theory. But instead of a reconciliation with the symbolic figure of the dead father, this act leads the narrator to a radical anti-Freudianism that, in the form of a refusal of the superego and its theory, expresses the major thesis of Sartre's philosophy with complete coherence: the access to liberty lies in refusal of the moral law and the annihilation of oneself in the other.

> The death of Jean-Baptiste was the central moment of my life. It put my mother back in fetters and gave me liberty. There is no good father, that is the rule; we ought not to reproach human beings, but rather the bond of parenthood, which is rotten. There is nothing better than making children; *having* them is a great iniquity. Had he lived, my father would have lain upon me at his full length, and would have crushed me. By chance he died young. Amid all the Aeneases bearing Anchises on their backs I pass from one bank to the other, alone and hating these invisible progenitors who sit astride their sons throughout their lifetimes. I left behind me a man who died young, who did not have time to be my father, and who today might be my child. Was this a good or an evil? I do not know; but I willingly accept the verdict of an eminent psychoanalyst: I have no superego.[48]

A reading of *Nausea* first, then *The Words*, and finally the *Freud* screenplay shows clearly that, if Sartre found a way to link the philosophy of concepts and the philosophy of the subject, he also found a way to embody in fiction a conceptuality that would never have attained such incandescence if it had only been conveyed in works of pure philosophy. But doubtless Sartre *also* had to be a philosopher to be capable in this way of making intimate obsessions that are never the pure illustration of a system of thought leap forth in his works of fiction. In *The Words* he wrote: "I was Roquentin, I depicted the warp of my own life in him, with no softening. At the same time I was myself, the chosen one, the analyst of hell. . . . Phony to the core, and mystified, I joyfully wrote about our unhappy condition. Dogmatic, I doubted all save that I was the chosen one of doubt. I restored with one hand what I destroyed with the other, and I regarded uneasiness as the guarantee of my security. I was happy."[49]

In this respect, this paradoxical and uneasy autobiography is one of the high points of twentieth-century literature. It pulverizes the rhetoric of intimate recital and of what is today called by the flat term "autofiction." With its purified and almost mystical style, this text, written entirely in the *passé simple* verb tense, as if the narrator were regarding his own birth, life, and death from the vantage point of the hell in which he has sunk his pen, or from that childhood which he exposes to public ridicule—this text impresses itself on the reader's unconscious, causing a symphony of signifiers to vibrate inside him, penetrating him in a strange and almost vampiresque fashion.

Sartre's *Words* is somehow fragments of memory, or portions of books, that direct every subject back to whatever consciousness she may have of her relation to herself and the world. And in this sense, in its quest for a ceaselessly interrupted subjectivity, this Sartrean autobiography, stripped clean of any tincture of the novelistic, bears a striking resemblance to a Freudian odyssey, with its origins in dreaming, its destiny in language, and its narrative support in nothingness. It is also the prototype of every first-person recital. This is why no one can read it without immediately yielding to the desire for a writing of the self repeated to infinity.

An astonishing reversal of "the childhood of a leader" and a fantastic exorcism![50] Like many of Sartre's projects, the *Freud* screenplay remained unfinished, primarily because Sartre and Huston were unable to produce a collaborative work. Moreover, there exist several versions of the text, and many still-unpublished drafts. The main reason, though, is that, once he withdrew his name from the film credits, Sartre tended to regard this interminable work as something of a castoff, good for nothing but a boost to his bank balance. When he was asked "were there works that you wrote primarily to earn money?" Sartre replied: "There were. I can think of one in any case. It was the *Freud* screenplay I wrote for Huston. I had just found out that I had no more money. I think it was when my mother had given me twelve million old francs to pay my taxes. They were paid, and I had no more debts, but I didn't have a sou either. Just then I was told that Huston wished to see me. He came round one morning and said, 'I am offering you 25 million to collaborate on a film about Freud.' I said yes and I got 25 million."[51]

From the point of view of the history of psychoanalysis, the Sartrean exorcism had the effect of desacralizing the body of Freud. Reading this screenplay twenty years after it was written (unfortunately it was published posthumously) and a century after the birth of Sartre, one is struck by the way it manages to free the real Freud from the rigid repetition of official history. If examples are needed, I could cite the admirable scenes in which Sartre makes the protagonist confront the hysterical woman's desire and then the Sartrean demon of transgression, or his portrayal of the moment at which Freud renounces sexual desire in order to gratify one stronger still: the desire to elucidate the sexual causes of desire. Never had any commentator on the Viennese saga succeeded so well in eroticizing the gesture with which Freud advances from error toward truth.

In choosing to show Freud at the moment at which he accomplishes the theoretical gesture that opens up the domain of the unconscious to modern thought, Sartre contradicts his own thesis, posited in *Being and Nothingness* and then in *Questions of Method*, to the effect that psychoanalysis has neither principle nor theoretical grounding. You could put it this way: through a Freud more Freudian than the original, Sartre in part renounces his own former anti-Freudian philosophical stance, and links a conceptual moment to an act of subjective liberty. Only in part, though, because this renunciation leads him to an even more radical anti-Freudianism, in which the only thing that counts is the welling up of a free and creative subject, stripped of any form of superego. This explains why, every time the question of psychoanalysis was raised, he tended to speak and act as if the event of the *Freud* screenplay had never taken place, as if the Freudian conceptual moment could never connect with the Sartrean act marked by subjective freedom.

In 1963, in a letter addressed to R. D. Laing and David Cooper, who had just published a study on him, Sartre extols the merits of an existential approach to mental illness, the only one capable, according to him, of humanizing psychiatry.[52] Without referring to Freud by name, he criticizes positivism and psychoanalysis in the best traditions of *Being and Nothingness*. Three years later, in the course of a violent clash with what he called "structuralism," Sartre once again brandished the torch of his existential Freudo-Marxism. He began by adopting a formula of Lacan, "the unconscious is the discourse of the other," which he regarded as clarifying Freud's ideas to a certain extent. But he immediately robbed it of its conceptual value by conceiving it in terms of intentionality and bad faith: "In these conditions—and to the extent that I am in agreement with Lacan—intentionality must be conceived as fundamental. There is no mental process that is not intentional, nor is there any that is not gummed up, betrayed, and deflected by language. But reciprocally, we are complicit in these betrayals, which constitute our depth."[53]

Sartre subsequently shifted into full polemical mode, indiscriminately charging Foucault, Althusser, and Lacan with a concerted refusal of history in the name of structure and a rejection of man for the sake of de-centering the subject. But those whom he regarded as the real specialists in structure, Claude Lévi-Strauss, Emile Benveniste, and Ferdinand de Saussure, were spared the full force of this blast. Though on this occasion he left out the name of Georges Dumézil, he did nevertheless acknowledge an authentic Freudian fidelity in Lacan. The approach here is the same as in *Being and Nothingness*, but it is structure that is accused, in 1966, of the sin once laid at the feet of Freudian psychoanalysis. And against structure Sartre mobilizes, in overblown fashion, a Marxist commitment that evokes the two extreme figures of the *Freud* scenario: the ultraleftism of Fliess and the bad faith of Meynert.

The episode of "the man with the tape recorder" [*l'homme au magnétophone*] is inscribed in an identical trajectory. This manuscript, published by *Les Temps Modernes* in 1969 and inspired by *The Sequestered of Altona*, has a well-known history. It features a patient who rebels against his analyst and insists on having a tape recorder running during their session, of which the text is supposedly a transcript. Despite the opposition of his two friends Jean-Bertrand Pontalis and Bernard Pingaud, Sartre decided to be really provocative; he claimed that he was emphasizing the irruption of the subject into the psychoanalyst's study and thus reversing the excessively univocal relation of the subject to the object: "I am not a false friend of psychoanalysis, but a critical fellow traveller. I have no wish—and for that matter no means—of ridiculing it. This dialogue will raise a smile: one always enjoys watching Guignol thrash the commissioner. Personally I don't find it amusing."[54]

Guignol doesn't actually succeed in thrashing the commissioner, but that doesn't mean that Sartre was not genuinely attempting to ridicule psychoanalysis. Why should he have denied himself this transgression? A year after the revolt of May 1968 he was seeing an expanding market in France for psychoanalysis (Lacanian and anti-Lacanian) catering especially to the social elite. This was something Gilles Deleuze also condemned, on the basis of a Freudo-Marxist theory of Reichian inspiration, as did Foucault through his unfailing support of Deleuze's position.[55] Sartre for his part relied on his own well-honed weapon, the ideal of the free subject, rather than desiring reason or the claim that Freudianism was drifting closer to repressive psychiatry. And though he was not blind to the derisory aspect of the false freedom of the man with the tape recorder, he continued to believe in the redemptive value of subjective freedom, the only true freedom there is. That is why he defended English antipsychiatry, itself inspired by his own philosophy, so stoutly. But this meant that the *Freud* screenplay, a genuine intellectual event, got buried even more deeply. Apparently he failed to see how much the publication at this time of this Faustian and nostalgic text could have done to elevate French Freudianism. It is easy to imagine the Lacanian generation of the 1970s (or a part of it at least), the generation that had been Sartrean at the time of the war of Algeria, being drawn to this screenplay, if only it had had the chance to read it during the author's lifetime.

I have had occasion, taking remarks made by Michel Foucault to Didier Eribon as my point of departure,[56] to reflect on the intertwined history of those two masters of freedom, Sartre and Lacan, who were confronted at around the same age with the French student revolt of May 1968, especially with Maoist radicalism. Sartre was caught up in the imaginary of revolution to the point of denying himself and was saved only by the writing of Flaubert, while Lacan entrenched himself in a species of baroque severity the better to understand, in the aftermath of verbal terror, the collapse of the militant ideal.

On one hand a Marat of sorts, with Girondin traits; on the other a species of Tocqueville with Thermidorian virtues. "Our alternating contemporaries," Michel Foucault called them. For the heirs of both the season had passed for saying with the Sartreans that the subject was radically free, or with the structuralists that he or she is determined by social or intrapsychic conditions. Better at this point to try to understand what lay hidden behind the very notion of subject—that complex and fragile thing of which it is difficult to speak, but without which there is no speaking.

What Foucault has to say is especially interesting because it appears to modify the stance he had taken in an interview with Madeleine Chapsal in 1966: "We experienced Sartre's generation as a generous and courageous one of course, with a passion for life, for politics, for existence; but we discovered something else for ourselves: the passion for concepts, and for what I would call system." And Foucault went on to emphasize in 1966 that his generation had broken with Sartre at the point when Lévi-Strauss on one hand and Lacan on the other (the former for societies, the latter for the unconscious) had shifted the primary goal of analysis from the mirroring of significations to the system that commanded them.[57]

That Foucault could thus oscillate between two passions, one for the philosophy of concepts and the other for the philosophy of commitment, before ultimately combining them in a unified project—and this can be traced in the unfolding of his own oeuvre—shows clearly that one cannot exist without the other. On condition, however, that they both serve to anchor a radical refusal of any philosophy of submission.

It is not in fact certain that, in terms of the generational lineage of the philosophers whose sources and critical influence I am trying to reconstruct, Sartre could have existed without Lacan. For the bond that symbolically unites them arises as much out of the history of the twentieth century as it does out of the philosophical filiation they created. Both were part of an antichauvinistic movement in the 1930s that authorized French thinkers to make a fresh approach to German philosophy. Neither was subsequently active in the Resistance, but during the course of the war both discovered, in the spectacle of a radical anti-Nazism to which they had not subscribed, the conditions for their own future thinking about the questions of commitment and freedom.

It is well known that soon after the liberation of France, in a celebrated text in response to *No Exit*, Lacan emphasized that man is not free to choose his chains because there does not exist any original welling up of freedom. Thus, in order to become free, he is condemned to integrate into the human collectivity by logical reasoning. In other words, only the fact of belonging to a group grounds the relation of the subject to the other, and only the virtue of logic leads man to truth, meaning to the acceptance of the other in accordance with a dialectic of recognition and misrecognition. So Lacan was taking his stance, in the Husserlian tradition and like Sartre, in favor of a philosophy of concepts into which he tried to integrate a nonsubjective philosophy of the subject, or as he put it, "an existential indetermination of the I."[58] Hence he made human liberty depend not on a logical choice escaping any psychology of the subject (as Georges Canguilhem does in relation to Cavaillès), but on a temporality: the temporality that authorizes every subject to submit to a logical decision when the "time for understanding" arrives.

That Sartre and Lacan were shaped by two of the major forces grounding our modernity—the Freudian revolution and the Marxist revolution—also shows that after having traversed the tempest of the war dreaming of a liberty for which they had not fought, they found the way to combine doctrinal adhesion with the spirit of dissent. Sartre was no more an orthodox communist or Marxist than Lacan was a legitimist Freudian. And it was thanks to this provocative stance, and it alone, that they became, for the generation of May 1968, masters capable of testing the limits of their own teachings. Having never had a word to say to each other while they were alive, either about the unconscious or the revolution, they left a shared silence as their legacy to a common posterity.

To that posterity it now falls to imagine a new Freud of the outset and a new Sartre of commitment, the one and the other torn free from error between a bordello and the shadowy banks of the Danube.

3. MICHEL FOUCAULT

{READINGS OF *HISTORY OF MADNESS*}

I N T H E Y E A R S F O L L O W I N G T H E P U B L I C A T I O N O F
History of Madness criticism of it by psychiatrists, psychologists, and
historians of psychopathology was both aggressive and ambivalent. Michel Foucault was denouncing all the ideals informing their knowledge,
shattering the *longue durée* of Philippe Pinel's humanitarianism, and declaring war on all varieties of institutional reformism: "This book did
not set out to do the history of mad folk alongside that of their counter-
parts, the reasonable folk, nor the history of reason in its opposition to
madness. The goal was to do the history of the incessant, ever-modified
division between them. . . . It was not medicine that defined the border
between reason and madness, but since the nineteenth century medical doctors have been charged with surveiling the frontier and standing
guard there. They signposted it with the term 'mental illness.' Indication
equals interdiction."[1]

Henri Ey immediately grasped the message.[2] An admirable clinician,
this theorist of organodynamism was also the last great representative
of alienism, the precursor of psychiatry. He laid claim to the tradition

of Philippe Pinel, and his experiment at the hospital of Bonneval, which had commenced between the two world wars, was very similar to that of the English Quaker William Tuke, one of the inventors of "moral treatment." It rested on the idea, originating in the philosophy of the Enlightenment, that there is always a remnant of reason in the madperson that allows a therapeutic relationship. But Ey's experiment also led to the creation of various residential institutions, including ones at Saint-Alban, Bonneuil, and the chateau of Laborde, that gave madpeople a greater degree of freedom, based on a community lifestyle, an absence of asylum-style restraints, and a Freudian valorization of the living word of the subject.

Inspired by Jacksonian neurology, from which Freud had borrowed certain concepts, the doctrine of organodynamism theorized by Henri Ey during the 1930s challenged the idea of a static organization of functions by emphasizing their hierarchical organization. It saw the psychic functions as dependent upon one another, in descending order. This doctrine ran counter to that of "constitutions" inherited from the German and French traditions. In this respect, the Jacksonian model was to Henri Ey what the Freudian model was to Jacques Lacan.

If Jackson had freed neurology from its mechanistic principles, Freud had abandoned neurology to found his theory of the unconscious and bring a new conception of madness to psychiatry. But according to Ey, it was necessary to align neurology with psychiatry in order to endow the latter with a theory capable of integrating Freudianism. In contrast Jacques Lacan's program, ever since his thesis of 1932,[3] was to renew Freud's gesture and rethink psychiatric knowledge on the model of the Freudian unconscious. Whereas Henri Ey was attempting, through a phenomenology of consciousness, to maintain the link between neurology and psychiatry, Jacques Lacan rejected both psychogenesis and organogenesis. Against them he proposed the notion of *psychogénie*, meaning a purely psychic organization of the personality. Both men shared the view that psychoanalysis must not serve as an auxiliary technique for the old psychiatry. In their eyes, Freud's discovery restored meaning to psychiatry in its rejection of the idea that nosology could be detached from the lived experience of madness, from its word. But they diverged in their attachment to organicism, which Ey included but Lacan excluded.

The conflict had broken out before the war, but it was starkly declared at the colloquy of Bonneval in 1946. At that time Lacan was preaching the necessity for a comprehensive return to Descartes as a way to think the essential causality of madness. In a few lines he offered a commentary on the famous words from book 1 of Descartes's *Meditations*, which would later be the bone of contention between Michel Foucault and Jacques Derrida: "And how could I deny that these hands and this body belong to me, unless perhaps I put myself in the same class as certain deranged persons whose brains are so troubled and clouded by the black vapors of bile that they constantly assert that they are kings when they are quite destitute, or that they are clad in gold and purple when they are quite naked, or who imagine that they are jugs, or that they have bodies made of glass? *Mais quoi!* These are madpeople, and I would be no less extravagant if I conducted myself on their example."[4]

Lacan was implying that the foundation by Descartes of the conditions of modern thought did not exclude the phenomenon of madness. This of course was a way of reaffirming the exclusively psychical character of the actual phenomenon, against Ey and the defenders of the dynamic psychiatry that originated with Philippe Pinel. That did not stop Lacan from declaring himself anti-Cartesian three years later in Zurich, before the assembled members of the International Psychoanalytical Association. He did so there to bolster his critique of the ego psychology then dominant, by emphasizing that the experience of psychoanalysis "is radically opposed to any philosophy issuing from the *cogito*."[5]

So on one hand Descartes was revendicated by Lacan for having conceived madness *with* the *cogito*. On the other, the *cogito* was disavowed for having given rise more or less to a non-Freudian psychology of the ego. Although Lacan was not a Foucauldian before Foucault, he was better prepared than the psychiatrists of his generation to accept the theses of *History of Madness*. Thanks to surrealism he had in fact fully integrated into his own method the idea that madness had its own logic and that it had to be considered apart from the traditional monologue brought to bear on it by psychiatric knowledge under the aegis of Cartesian reason. These were not the views of Ey and his group at *L'Évolution Psychiatrique*.

From 1961 Henri Ey spent a number of years pondering Foucault's book, which he qualified as "psychiatricidal." Yet he saw so clearly that this philosopher turned historian of science and medicine was doing something important that he decided to dedicate an entire meeting of his association to the "ideological conception of the history of madness." It took place at Toulouse in December 1969. Foucault refused to attend, about which Ey had this to say:

> This is a psychiatricidal position so pregnant with consequences for the very idea of man that we would very much have wished that Michel Foucault could attend. Both to pay him the rightful tribute of our admiration for the systematic methodology of his thinking, and to contest the idea that mental illness can be considered the marvellous manifestation of madness, or even in exceptional cases as the very spark of poetic genius. For it is something quite different to a cultural phenomenon! Although some among us, made uncomfortable by the vulnerability of their own positions, or seduced by the brilliant paradoxes of Foucault, might have preferred not to have such a debate, I for my part regret the lack of a direct confrontation. Michel Foucault, whom I was at pains to invite, writes to me that he regrets it as much as I do and apologizes for being unable to be at Toulouse at this time. So we shall proceed as if he were here. In the clash of ideas, it matters little whether those who, precisely, are engaged exclusively in intellectual combat are physically present.[6]

The fact that Foucault's theses partially overlapped with those of the contemporary antipsychiatry movement made it both complex and hazardous to defend psychiatric knowledge. The antipsychiatry movement had launched its critique of the notion of mental illness and its charge that psychiatry was itself pathogenic in 1959, though the path it followed was quite different from that taken by the author of *History of Madness*.

In England, California, and Italy opposition to psychiatry arose on the terrain of the asylum and political practice, and it occupied a space there much like the space occupied in France by the enlightened dynamism of Henry Ey, by the institutional psychotherapy flowing from the pioneering experiment at the hospital of Saint-Alban (where Georges Canguilhem had been active), and by the Lacanian renewal. The antipsychiatry movement took root in countries where psychoanalysis had been "normalized" into a neo-Freudian dogma and where dynamic psychiatry had evolved into a rigid organicism.

The dissenters were all characterized, moreover, by their commitments to the anticolonial struggle, multiculturalism, and extreme left militancy. Gregory Bateson was an anthropologist and vigorously culturalist; David Cooper was a psychiatrist and had fought against apartheid in South Africa; Franco Basaglia was a member of the Italian Communist Party. As for R. D. Laing, he had become a psychoanalyst after having practiced psychiatry in the British army in India. For these rebels, madness was not an illness at all, but a *history*: the history of a voyage, of a passage or a situation, with schizophrenia as its most completely realized form, inasmuch as it translated the malaise of social or familial alienation into a delirious response.

Thus the antipsychiatrists shared with Foucault the idea that madness had to be thought of as a history, the archives of which had been repressed through a formidable conspiracy, as alienism evolved into psychiatry and reason evolved into oppression. But whereas the antipsychiatrists intended to be pure practitioners, utilizing the tools of Sartrean philosophy and cultural anthropology to dismantle all institutional norms, Foucault remained a theorist, a philosopher, a militant of intellectuality. He fought for the emergence of a history of madness but did not go to live among madpeople.

And he relied upon the most impetuous works of Bataille and Nietzsche in forcing this "damned part" of Western reason, irreducible to any form of discursive mastery, to emerge into view.[7] Hence the combat in which he engaged, with and against historians, to give voice to the transgressive archive—meaning to the raw and hallucinatory document, the infamous text, the trace not of the expert, judge, or censor, but of the madman, criminal, and assassin.

The historians of psychiatry condemned Michel Foucault for his Promethean attitude. Quite properly. Not only had he stolen away the object of their desire, he was also threatening to render their position in society otiose. From the time psychiatry had become a domain of knowledge, it had told its own history in terms of the purest hagiography: the glorious deeds and gestures of the masters were in general related by the most respectful pupil, who was guaranteed in advance, when he himself became a master, of seeing his own favorite pupil repeat the eulogy that he himself had pronounced at the moment when he succeeded to his own master. The very opposite of imparting fresh life to a heritage through a farewell, or a ceremony of farewell. Thus there had been forged, in a sphere of pure transmission of power, a pious history in which, from Salpêtrière to Charenton by way of Bicêtre, a legendary gallery of portraits followed one after the other whose only function was to lead back to the illustrious progenitor: Philippe Pinel.

Pinel was a pure myth, and everyone knew that the myth had been invented by Étienne Esquirol during the Restoration solely in order to remake the founding hero into an anti-Jacobin humanitarian and so bury the fact that he had been appointed to the hospital at Bicêtre by a decree of the Montagnard Convention on 11 September 1793. The myth of the unsullied and irreproachable hero had then been handed down from generation to generation in a canonical form that no longer bore any relation to historical reality. But like all myths, it had become truer than reality. It went like this:

Under the Terror, Pinel received a visit from Couthon, who was looking for suspects among the mad inmates. All trembled at the sight of Robespierre's faithful follower, who had left his paralytic's chair and was carried by manservants. Pinel led him past the cells, where the sight of the agitated inmates made him intensely fearful, as they heaped injuries on him. Couthon turned to the alienist and said to him: "Citizen, are you mad yourself, to wish to set animals such as these at liberty?" The doctor replied that it was all the harder to treat deranged persons when they were deprived of fresh air and freedom. So Couthon agreed that the chains should be removed, but warned Pinel about his presumptuousness. He was then carried back to his carriage, and the philanthropist set about his work: he released the mad ones from their chains, and thus gave birth to alienism.[8]

In 1961, when Michel Foucault's book appeared, this pious history had been relegated to the attic, and the community of historians of psychiatry had adopted a modern method in its place, one partly inspired by the work of Canguilhem and partly by the influence of the founders of the Annales school. So they set about studying the history of the conceptual tools proper to psychiatry and to its various nosological constructs. Attempts were even made to show that the story did not begin with Pinel but was part of the gradual, and very long-term, adventure of the laborious emergence of the notion of mental illness.

Madness, it was said, was natural to man, and had been so since time immemorial. Through steady evolution, it had been rescued from the gaze cast on it by magical thought and had become an object of science. The thrust of this was that the apprehension of madness—its comprehension—had gone from obscurantism to progress, from religion to humanism, from nature to culture—and from culturalism to universalism. The emphatic message was that man is a creature of reason, and that, in the end, a modern psychiatrist fully instructed in Freudianism and versed in ethnology, is always preferable to a witch doctor, an illusionist, or an inquisitor. Better, it was said, the justice of magistrates than medieval torture; better the moral treatment of Pinel than the "ship of fools."

And then, just when the history of psychiatry had made itself presentable by giving up its old cherished hagiography, along came a man, neither a psychiatrist nor a historian, claiming to reduce all the efforts of the specialists in psychopathology to nothing at one stroke by engaging in a pure game of structural displacement. What he was saying in substance was that instead of asserting that the birth of a conceptual arsenal allows us to account for the presence of madness in human nature, I will undertake to show that this arsenal has been constructed upon the retroactive illusion that madness was already a given in nature. From that standpoint, madness is not a fact of nature but one of culture, and its history is that of the cultures that label it and persecute it.

And so medical science takes its turn as one of the historical forms of the relation of madness to reason. Its concepts are inadequate to analyzing this relation, and that is why, if we are to grasp its meaning, we must begin by setting aside those concepts. Georges Canguilhem, who had agreed to act as the rapporteur of Foucault's thesis, understood right away that this was a radical revision of the psychiatric manner of thinking about madness: "It is thus the significance of the beginnings of positivist psychiatry, before the Freudian revolution, that is studied in Foucault's work. And through psychiatry, it is the significance of the arrival of positive psychology that finds itself revised. Such a casting into doubt of the 'scientific' status of psychology will not be the least of the reasons for the surprise that this study will provoke."[9]

With these statements Canguilhem once again took to task the false science he so abhorred and that he never ceased to regard as a technology of submission. Psychology was represented on the examining board for the thesis by Daniel Lagache, who felt, with perfect justice, that he was being given rough treatment. For Foucault's gesture was ruining the work to which he had devoted his university career: the unity of psychology. However he refrained from challenging the young philosopher on theoretical grounds and contented himself with pointing out errors of detail: gaps in information or negligence concerning the conceptual armature of psychoanalysis.

Historians working in the field were not slow to criticize the book, while acknowledging that it had given them food for thought they had not been expecting. Indeed, one could measure the intrusive force of the Foucauldian event of 1961 by the strength of the resistance it aroused. The most positive critics tried to counter the fracas of this structural reversal by listing, at interminable length, all the author's mistakes. And God knows they found them: wrong dates, errors of interpretation, errors in the selection of documents, ignorance of some important event and exaggerated emphasis on some other that Foucault had chosen to feature, and so on.

Foucault was charged, in short, with having hallucinated a history of madness that did not figure in the archives of the history of psychiatry. And in truth, it did not figure there. For at the heart of this history he had *seen* something that the historians of psychiatry were unable to see, and in order to force this invisible and unnameable thing out into the open, he had had to invent, taking his cue from Freud, an unrecorded primal scene, the mythical scene of the notorious original and ever-recurrent— and ever-unconditional—division. The division between unreason and madness, the division between the menacing madness of the paintings of Bosch and the tame folly of Erasmus's discourse, the division between a critical consciousness (in which madness becomes illness) and a tragic consciousness (in which it self-sublimates into creation, as in Goya, Van Gogh, or Antonin Artaud). This series culminated with another, more insidious division that Foucault had to invent, the one internal to the Cartesian *cogito*: madness, he was saying, is excluded from thought at the very moment at which it ceases to pose a threat to the prerogatives of thought.

So, like the psychiatrists and the psychologists, the historians of psychopathology took the view that this madness, which they had been unable to discern in the archives and which Foucault appeared to have magically exhumed, was in the nature of a brilliant but irresponsible literary construct. In their view, the "madness" he had conjured up like a specter or phantom remained foreign to the reality of the suffering of the "real" patients whom psychiatrists had in their charge and whose sad epic it was the business of historians to relate.

Consequently they accused the man Foucault of being neither physician nor psychiatrist nor psychologist, and of never having dealt with real inmates in an asylum, ordinary madpeople, hateful agitated and stupid, or vice versa gentle, docile, controlled, and reasonable. Did a philosopher with so little clinical experience have the right to transform the anonymous madness of real mental patients into this sublime fresco? Did he have the right to transfigure the ordinary inmate of the ordinary asylum into a sublime poet (Artaud) or a painter of genius (Van Gogh)? Foucault, they said, enjoys mocking honest hospital practitioners faced with the enormous chore of restraining patients every day.[10]

Another version went like this: why is this elegant philosopher, a doctor's son, so interested in madness when he did not even choose to follow a career in psychiatry? Why so much violence and rebellion? Why such transgression? Was this individual not perhaps possessed by an experience of deviance that caused him to identify with imaginary madpeople, the better to mark himself off from a corporation he had chosen not to join? It was known that Foucault had contemplated suicide, that he was homosexual, that he had tried psychoanalysis for three weeks, and finally that he had visited the patients at the Saint-Anne hospital and had attended a number of presentations of mental patients for his diploma in psychopathology. The conclusion drawn was that his book was in part the disguised autobiography of a pervert, in part the disguised confession of a mentally ill person afflicted with melancholy.[11]

Arguments like these allowed the adversaries of Foucault's thesis to ignore the place that his iconoclastic book held both in its author's personal itinerary and in the history of the ways of recounting madness. The text had been almost entirely written in the mists of the city of Uppsala and completed "in the great stubborn sunshine of Polish freedom."[12] And if Foucault did introduce into it that damned part of the lived experience of madness, so often repressed by the discourse of psychopathology, that is doubtless because he had experienced in his own being the principle of division that his book featured: the division between consciousness of the gaze cast upon madness and the absolute withdrawal of any gaze. In other words, in his passage from the mists of Uppsala to the sunshine of Warsaw, the philosopher had reached the core of madness without giving up his stance as a scientist. But prior to making this great voyage he had gone through a sort of intimate and tenebrous storm that had come close to leading him down "the pathways of night." "A great Husserlian ascesis led me into regions so strange and so unimagined that I do not know if it is possible to breathe here. After having hesitated whether to become a monk, or to turn off down the pathways of night, I decided to force myself to live here. But I am only just starting to draw breath."[13]

So it is no coincidence that, thirty-four years later, another philosopher recalled this Foucauldian crossing when he came to write the history of his own madness. Louis Althusser wrote: "Even though I was released from psychiatric confinement two years ago, I remain, for the public to whom I am known, one of the *disappeared*. Neither dead nor alive, still unburied but 'unemployed'—Foucault's magnificent word to designate madness: *disappeared*. . . . One of the disappeared may startle public opinion by turning up again (as I am now doing) in the broad daylight of life . . . in the great sunshine of Polish freedom."[14]

At Uppsala, where he got a job as an instructor in French in August 1955 thanks to Georges Dumézil, an archive of impressive bulk was available to Foucault: that deposited at the Carolina Rediviva library by Dr. Erik Waller. Twenty-one thousand documents: letters, manuscripts, rare books, and obscure works, as well as a considerable collection of medical treatises on the maladies of the soul, the treatment of the deranged, the law governing hospitals and charitable institutions. For the period of the French Revolution he could turn to the classics: Doublet and Colombier, Tenon, Brissot, Cabanis, Pinel, the reports of the Committee on Mendicancy, and finally the four volumes of documents edited by Alexandre Tuetey on public assistance in Paris.

But since this collection lacked archives from hospitals and places of incarceration, which would have made it possible to *quantify* the *longue durée* of institutional confinement, Foucault's adversaries were quick to assert that he had dodged giving a true historical account of his topic, because the archives at his disposal, however rich, did not reveal the *true* truth of the *true* history of *true* confinement, which as far as they were concerned was simply a succession of imperceptible small events spread out across several centuries.

What's the point, they said, of resorting to overwrought rhetorical turns like *grande renfermement* [great confinement], *conjuration* [conspiracy], or *partage* [division, sharing] as ways of describing what came down, in the end, to chronology pure and simple? Another version went: if Foucault focused so much on the twenty-one thousand documents in the Carolina, that's because they supported the hypotheses born of his own imagination, to which he had decided in advance to cling.

The first to go after him was Stirn Lindroth, who held the chair in history of ideas and science at Uppsala, and with whom Foucault had intended to defend his thesis. Alarmed by the unacademic style of the impetuous young man, Lindroth judged both his writing and his hypotheses to be too far-fetched; he would even make it his boast, many years later, that he had not perceived the novelty of the book.[15]

As for the polemic about archival sources orchestrated by the French specialists, it had less to do with the manner in which Foucault had utilized them than it did with the fashion in which the historians of psychopathology were willing or unwilling to see that their world was collapsing around their ears. When *History of Madness* appeared, they had as yet produced nothing capable of seriously challenging it. Henri Ellenberger's *History of the Discovery of the Unconscious*, the first great founding text of psychiatric and psychoanalytic historiography, written from a perspective both positivist and Annalist, was still in gestation and would only appear in English in 1970, nine years after Foucault's *History*.

Without having read *History of Madness*, which he was later to characterize as "obscure," Ellenberger did share with Foucault the idea that madness was a fact of culture. But he did not perceive the nature/culture divide in the same way as the philosopher did. In his eyes, madness was certainly "natural" to man, but was only perceptible as such through the diversity of its ethnic manifestations. From this perspective it may well have existed from time immemorial, but it had only become comprehensible on the day that man acquired the ability to apprehend it, first through magical thinking and later through rational interpretation.

In 1961 the historians of psychopathology had indeed abandoned the terrain of hagiography, but from the historiographical point of view, the Foucauldian gesture hit them too soon for them to be able to hit back with a constituted body of knowledge and too late for them to be able to invalidate him by denying his pathbreaking status. Thus they were forced to register his existence, consciously or unconsciously, but always at the cost of a negative assessment: the philosopher was a master, agreed, but he was a perverse one; his book might be pathbreaking, but it was also faulty and destructive.

Between 1954 and 1961 Michel Foucault had altered his stance. In his first theoretical work, *Mental Illness and Psychology*, published in 1954, he showed that the genesis of modern forms of alienation had to be understood on the basis of figures from antiquity: the "energumen" of the Greeks, the *mente captus* of the Latins, the "demoniac" of the Christians.[16] At that time, therefore, he adopted an evolutionist attitude toward his object of study, madness. This is the stance his detractors would later accuse him of abandoning. He saw the concept of mental illness as the terminal phase of a way of looking at madness that had begun in antiquity and had passed through the medieval notion of "divine possession." So in 1954 his presupposition was that alienation had been permanent throughout history, whereas in 1961 he relinquished any idea of continuity in favor of a system of divisions based on the exclusion of madness by reason.[17] At the same time he rejected the notion of mental toolkit, which had ended up poisoning the research of the heirs of the Annales school by steering them into the search for an undiscoverable "period mentality"—something more like the idea that every ethnic group has its own psychology than a method for the constructive reinterpretation of the past.[18]

This radical shift showed clearly that Foucault was aware that madness could have a history configured differently from the one he was constructing in Uppsala. But he could not think that history at the same time as the other: the object of his research was not the psychological definition of mental illness but the quest for an ontological truth of madness. Hence the imperative need for a revision.

The most telling attack on *History of Madness* was dealt by Gladys Swain. Sixteen years after its publication, she faulted its author for having taken literally the myth of Pinel's abolition of the shackles, without trying to find out what lay beneath it. And indeed Foucault had never dwelt on the matter. Although he knew that Pinel had never carried out this gesture, although he was not ignorant of the role the attendant Pussin had played in the gradual freeing of the deranged inmates, although he knew that the encounter between Pinel and Couthon had never taken place, he regarded the myth as true because, in his system of structural divisions, it stood for the foundational act of alienism.

In thus revendicating the foundational power of myth, he was proceeding in the manner of Sartre, who was contemporaneously reinventing, in complete disregard of archival research, a Freud of his own, truer than the true Freud, tormented by doubt, and shot through with a sort of Nietzschean Sturm und Drang.

Gladys Swain contested this approach, focusing on the origins of the modern asylum in the nineteenth century. She showed that psychiatry was born, not with an act—necessarily mythic—of setting the deranged free, but with the attribution to the alienist of powers formerly exercised by attendants. The myth of the abolition of the shackles thus served to get Pussin out of the way and allow Esquirol to dominate the asylum and nosology in the name of a totemic ancestor turned object of hagiography: Philippe Pinel.[19]

This ancestor Swain proposed to historicize, abandoning myth-making so as to understand who he had really been and what he had accomplished. Foucault of course did not address this question because he refused to situate himself on that terrain. Yet Gladys Swain's approach owed everything to Foucault's, for it lay in redirecting toward psychiatric discourse the interrogations that the philosopher had formulated with respect to the language of madness. It was thus *against* Foucault that she brought into focus a new problematic for the history of psychiatry—that of the genesis of the asylum—but at the cost of being unable clearly to recognize how much her argumentation owed to the Foucauldian gesture.

Three years after the publication of *The Subject of Madness*, Gladys Swain collaborated with Marcel Gauchet on a book dedicated to "moral treatment" and the genesis of the asylum from Pinel to Esquirol, *The Practice of the Human Spirit*.[20] Foucault's theses were not explicitly refuted in it, but the authors aimed to demonstrate that the history of modern societies was dictated by a logic of integration resting on the postulate of egalitarianism. In consequence this history could not be understood according to a model of the exclusion of alterity. In the hierarchical and inegalitarian societies that preceded the French classical age, said Swain and Gauchet, the madman was only tolerated because he was regarded either as subhuman (a mindless beast) or as suprahuman (divinely possessed): between the animalesque and the godlike. In modern societies, democratic and egalitarian, a reversal had come about: the madman was no longer regarded as the excluded Other but as the alter ego, that is, as an ill subject.

The two authors were carrying on the work begun by Swain three years earlier: work at once different from Foucault's, since it portrayed the nineteenth-century asylum as the realization of a democratic utopia, yet perfectly inscribed in the aftermath of *History of Madness*, since it tended to demonstrate how the madperson had undergone a metamorphosis by the fact of being integrated into the psychiatric institution.

It is indeed the case that Foucault had never sought to depict the asylum as the realization of a democratic utopia. Nor had he ever sought to demonstrate how it was that this utopia contained within itself its own proper failure, meaning the failure of the asylum and of "moral treatment." Why? Quite simply because this—highly interesting—thesis depended on a continuist obviousness from which he had cut loose in 1960. He had constructed his system of divisions not to counter it but to emphasize how every epoch organizes its utopia, in other words its gaze upon madness. From that perspective, to bring out the recurring alterity of madness in the history of human societies was to throw into sharp relief the utopian aspect of every view of madness.

Far from criticizing Foucault's work, Gladys Swain and Marcel Gauchet acknowledged his pathbreaking status. Nevertheless, in their preface they accorded greater prominence to *The Will to Knowledge*,[21] which came out in 1976, than they did to *History of Madness*: the former was qualified as a "central" work and the latter as an "indirectly central" one, already relegated to the past. But above all, the two authors preceded the recognition thus accorded Foucault with a formidable assault on Freud's discoveries, which were exposed to the charge of participating "fully in a logic of totalitarianism." As for the partisans of a "return to Freud," they too found themselves stigmatized as Jacobins of 1793, *already* Bolsheviks without knowing it, and so *already* Stalinists without being aware of it.

In other words, without ever mentioning the names of Freud or Lacan, Swann and Gauchet calmly informed readers in the 1980s that the so-called Freudian revolution was no more than a totalitarian revival of the Jacobin revolution of sinister memory. Indeed, as far as they were concerned, it was simply the foundational act of the abominable Gulag to come.

These far-fetched views, inspired by those of François Furet concerning the French Revolution,[22] disregarded the fact that the teaching and practice of psychoanalysis had always been prohibited by dictatorships, beginning with the one set up by the Nazis, who characterized it as a "Jewish science," and then by the Stalinists, who made it a "bourgeois science." The authors, ever vigilant in their critique of the "mistakes" of Foucault, appeared to forget that a number of representatives of this totalitarian discipline had been persecuted, exterminated, and tortured on account of their ideas, sometimes for that matter with the tacit complicity of other psychoanalysts.

But what was a preface of this kind doing anyway in a scholarly work of five hundred pages entirely dedicated to the history of the asylum, with which neither Freud, nor Lacan, nor psychoanalysis, nor even the history of psychoanalysis, had anything to do?

If Swain and Gauchet preferred *The Will to Knowledge* to *History of Madness*, that was because in the later book Foucault saluted the critiques of Freudianism advanced by Gilles Deleuze and Félix Guattari. In their *Anti-Oedipus* of 1972 these two had carried on the tradition of Wilhelm Reich by setting a theory of desiring fluxes, alien to any form of symbolic representation, against a Freudian system they characterized as repressive and "Oedipal."[23] And as well as Freud, it was the doctrine of Lacan that Deleuze and Guattari were targeting, on account of its drift into dogmaticism and logicality.

In 1961, in *History of Madness*, Foucault inscribed Freud's discovery in the internal continuity of the history of psychopathology, though he was always careful to show its status of alterity too. He clearly demonstrated the connection between Freud and Pierre Janet, while continually asserting the obvious radical discontinuity between the two doctrines. In 1976 in *The Will to Knowledge* he was no longer dealing with the same problem, choosing instead to focus on the internal continuity linking the techniques of confession and avowal to that of psychoanalysis. And in this perspective, the theses of Deleuze and Guattari helped him to formulate his own.

As for psychoanalysis, far from considering it a totalitarian enter-prise, Foucault emphasized its remoteness from any such outlook. Freud had broken away from theories of heredity and degeneration and had chosen to emphasize the role of sexuality in reaction to the terrible up-surge of racism that was occurring in his time: "the Law—the law of the alliance, of forbidden consanguinity, of the Father-Sovereign." In sum, he had convoked the ancient order of power around the question of de-sire. And Foucault added: " Thanks to that, psychoanalysis has been—in essence, and with a few exceptions—opposed to fascism in theory and practice."[24]

This assessment by Foucault, with which I completely concur, was meant to apply to the discipline itself. For it is the disciplinary essence of psychoanalysis that is incompatible with fascist dictatorship and all the forms of discrimination associated with it: racism, anti-Semitism, xeno-phobia. The behavior of certain representatives of psychoanalysis who, in certain precise historical circumstances, willingly collaborated with regimes that were aiming to eradicate it, is another matter.[25]

By referring to *The Will to Knowledge* rather than to *History of Mad-ness*, Swain and Gauchet were able to cite Foucault as if he were an anti-Freudian, sweeping aside his inaugural work and propping up a positiv-ist doctrine in its place. Only this, it was claimed, would henceforth have the power to account seriously not just for madness, but for the "subject" of madness: the alienated individual of democratic societies. For that matter, their virulent attack on putatively "totalitarian" psychoanalysis was also aimed at the Lacanian reading of the work of Freud, inasmuch as Lacan, like Foucault, and for fifty years, had been engaged in deep reflection of the nature of madness. And at a time when his doctrine was being made to look ridiculous by the sectarian behavior of a number of his partisans, the best way to damage Lacan was to pass the extravagant master off as a vicious Stalinist brute, in other words (the supreme insult for these two authors) as a Jacobin of 1793.

This attempted abolition showed clearly that, twenty years after its publication, *History of Madness* was still poisoning the spirit of all who were promoting a new history of psychopathology by claiming to be more democratic than Foucault—to whom suspicion always clung of excessive sympathy for the shipwrecked ones of the night and an ambition to be the dark originator of a colossal philosophy of rebellion that might undermine the ideals of a psychology in the service of the norm.

In short, Swain and Gauchet demonized Freud's discoveries so as to deny *History of Madness* its historical impact and supply the artisans of psychopathological thought with a tool they could use in its place. But there is no getting round it: This attempt to eradicate Foucauldian and Freudian thought has been a complete failure. In France and everywhere else.

And it may well be that the specter of defeat now facing the detractors of Foucault's thought is the consequence of their belief in a purely organicist conception of madness, a conception dominated by psychopharmacology and behavioralism, with no connection any more to Pinel, or to nosology, or to madness, or to any utopia—only to a complete absence of thought. From this perspective, the book by Swain and Gauchet was just the inaugural phase of this absence of thought. All the more so in that by assigning a unique function to the asylum—that of being linked to a democratic utopia—the two authors register its gradual disappearance, and thus its slowly programmed end.

The only thing left for them to do, in order to think this end and the end of all thought, was to revive the merits of empirical pluralism—which Gladys Swain did in 1987, in designating a single possible line of conduct for psychiatry, the most conformist one imaginable: the medicalization of existence on one hand, the taking of the psychological subject into society's charge on the other.[26]

At the same moment, two representatives of a philosophy of submission, Alain Renaut and Luc Ferry, who posed as the slayers of a putative "1968 thought" invented by terrorist thinkers hostile to the France of the Enlightenment, were also busy casting *History of Madness*, explicitly this time, into the hell of a new totalitarianism, no longer Jacobin but Nietzschean-Heideggerian.[27] Their book, which enjoyed much success under the title *1968 Thought*, made no attempt to state in what respect Foucault really was a Nietzschean, nor what he might have derived from his reading of the works of Heidegger. Far from it! The term "1968 thought" was simply utilized as a set phrase to signify that Foucault had moved—along with other Freudian, Nietzschean, or Heideggerian bit players like Jacques Derrida, Jacques Lacan, and Pierre Bourdieu—from one totalitarianism to another: from Bolshevik Jacobinism to Nazism.

Bolstering their case with reference to the five hundred pages of Swain and Gauchet's *Practice of the Human Spirit*, which, the reader will recall, deals exclusively, except for the preface, with the scholarly study of the asylum in the nineteenth century, the two philosophers accused Foucault of being both obscurantist and antidemocratic. Obscurantist because he preferred the "ship of fools" (called "inegalitarian") to the chemical straitjacket (called "egalitarian"). Antidemocratic because he chose not to see that the modern asylum responded not so much to a logic of exclusion as to a democratic utopia, that is to say, a project to integrate madness through "moral treatment" that contained the seed of its own failure.

So in 1986, twenty-five years after the publication of *History of Madness* and two years after Foucault's death, he was being accused of a crime he had not committed by imputing to him a project that was never his. Claiming that his system of divisions was just the result of a "Nietzschean-Heideggerian" preference that elevated the age of medieval witchcraft and magic above the age of Tocqueville and the straitjacket, they decked him out in the extravagant cassock of a nihilist prophet on a mission to wreck the two great pillars of our modern societies: science and democracy.

It is quite true that Foucault took sides in the combats inspired by his book and the antipsychiatry movement, supporting the various alternative networks hostile to psychiatric power, especially the biopower of the experts who were poisoning democratic society. But that did not mean that he acquiesced when his theses were reduced to simplistic slogans. Over the course of the struggles in which he engaged, he showed himself to be a man of dialogue, always preferring debate to spontaneous acts of rebellion. When it came to psychiatry, he readily took a reformist line. No doubt this was his way of taking a playful distance from his own prose, which did indeed vibrate with real insurrectional violence.

It is because they have overlooked the harm done by this biopower, and carried along by Gauchet's ideas, have yoked themselves to the principles of that police-headquarters psychology denounced by Canguilhem, that certain sociologists, philosophers, psychoanalysts, and psychiatrists have today made themselves into servants of an ideology of assessment. When they maintain, for example, that the probing of the subject through cerebral imaging might finally bring a solution to all of mankind's metaphysical interrogations,[28] or when they suggest that any truly scientific historiography must rid itself of any form of "heroic" representation, one inevitably recalls Michel Foucault denouncing "the indignity of power, from infamous sovereignty down to ridiculous authority."[29]

It has to be said: Anglophone scholarship, in the person of Jan Goldstein, produced the real history of French psychiatry in the nineteenth century, which those who were blaming Foucault for being unable to initiate had dreamed of turning out themselves. Impressed by the inept accusations of Gauchet, Ferry, and Renaut, and permanently terrified at the thought that the philosopher himself might direct one of his caustic imprecations their way, the French upholders of this sociopsychology of measurable subjectivity produced nothing of interest in this respect, whereas Foucault's oeuvre has spread throughout the world, continuing to stimulate new interpretations of madness, the body, sex, desire, and power.[30]

Focusing on the birth and evolution of psychiatry in France from the end of the eighteenth century down to the dawn of the twentieth (from Pinel to Charcot), Goldstein kept aloof in 1987 from the disputes occasioned in France by the publication of Foucault's master work.[31]

Neither letting herself be overwhelmed by it nor wasting time sifting it for "mistakes," Jan Goldstein frankly acknowledged once and for all the importance of *History of Madness* for the area of her own research. Foucault had reversed the gaze directed at madness, raised questions about the incarceration of madpeople, and identified a division between reason and unreason at the core of human subjectivity and Western society.

Starting with that, she accomplished the tour de force of writing a total history of psychiatry over the course of a century: its salient theoretical issues, its concepts, its professionalization, its clinical classifications, its social and political actors (doctors, intellectuals, patients, criminals).

Overall, an engrossing narrative, with the scenery of Balzac's novels in the background: the Revolution, the empire, the restoration, the July monarchy. Goldstein showed how a medicine of the psyche was able to impose itself as an interpretive framework for human behavior, then generalize itself over all Western societies.

To *console* and to *classify*: The two verbs of her title referred to the two major functions of psychiatric knowledge, poised between religion and science. The alienist of the late eighteenth century was at first the successor of the priest, and his role was indeed to *console* the patient. Support and compassion were his main virtues. Once secularized, mental illness was no longer linked to demonic possession. The madman escaped the exorcists, and it was the doctor turned psychiatrist who provided him with care and received the avowal of his suffering.

But the psychiatrist had equally to combat religious obscurantism. A man of the Enlightenment, he defended the values of science. Thus he had to be capable, not simply of classifying illnesses, but of *classifying* the mental universe of the subject, in other words of inventing classifications able to convey the new order of the world and give effect to the new desire to integrate the madman into the juridical space created by the Declaration of the Rights of Man and of the Citizen.

The book opens in 1778 with the creation of the Société Royale de Médecine, of which the permanent secretary was the celebrated Félix Vicq d'Azir, the author in 1790 of a *New Plan for the Constitution of Medicine in France*. The ideas of Cabanis and the group known as the Ideologues inspired Vicq d'Azir to combine medicine with the new science of man: anthropology. Politically his goal was to break with the feudal system of corporations and create a state medical system.

The new medical art, the triumph of which was assured by the Revolution and the empire, was linked to a materialist theory, psychophysiology, which opposed the ancient spiritual conception of the soul's divine essence preached by religion. For scientific medicine, man was a totality formed of a body and a psyche, but this psyche was purely a manifestation of physiology.

In 1792 the former university faculties were abolished and the medical profession was defined as a liberal art. In 1803 François Antoine Fourcroy, a pupil of Vicq d'Azir, spearheaded the creation of state medical schools charged with controlling what was taught. The new profession had the privilege of self-regulation, however, and this was the defining feature of the notion of "liberal profession" as we know it today. Borrowed from Adam Smith, it assumed the existence of a clear separation between the sphere in which the state was competent and the exercise of freedoms. All who did not fit into this new order could be regarded as charlatans and penalized for practicing medicine illegally.

Psychiatry came into being within this context, as a medical specialty.[32] Philippe Pinel became the organizer of this new outlook on madness, which joined the art of *consoling* and the faculty of *classifying*. Consolation as conceived by Pinel was "moral treatment," a mixture of physical care and techniques of gentle restraint and persuasion grounded in the idea that the madman could be cured because a remnant of reason still existed inside him. The key work of classification was Pinel's *Medico-Philosophical Treatise on Mental Alienation, or Mania*, published in 1800.

This work defined the categories of mental illness that were to serve as the framework of psychiatric knowledge for a century. As on every occasion of clinical refoundation, a new term was employed to indicate the essence of madness: *manie* [mania]. The Pinelian madman was above all a maniac, afflicted with furor and acute delirium, a man right out of the trauma of the Revolution.

After describing the birth of Pinelian psychiatry, Jan Goldstein analyzes the theoretical and political debates that took place during the Restoration and the July monarchy. These led to the passing of the law of 1838, allowing state asylums to be created—with psychiatric hospitals gradually being built throughout France—and the status of the deranged individual, within a bourgeois society devoted to commerce and the protection of the family ideal, to be defined.

Once again a key term served to focus discussion about the nature of madness: now it was *monomanie* [monomania] instead of *manie*. Coined in 1810 by Étienne Esquirol, the founder of the asylum and himself a pupil of Pinel, this category became the paradigm of madness until around 1850. The term "monomania" designated the obsession, the fixed idea that could fasten on a healthy mind. Above all, though, it betrayed the change of mentality that had occurred at the heart of a society built on regicide. The monomania attributed to the Esquirolian madman was simply the pathological version of the "normal" ambition proper to postrevolutionary society, a society where every individual now had the right and the means to set himself up as a king or an emperor—the king of perfumery, the king of finance, the emperor of crime, and so on—a society right out of Balzac's *Comedie humaine*, with its Vautrins, its Nuncingens, its César Birotteaus.

The notion of monomania was at stake in another battle, this one between jurists and alienists. As psychiatric knowledge built up its own stable institutional structure, it attempted to extend the notion of madness to all criminal acts. Hence Esquirol's creation in 1825 of the expression *manie homicide* [homicidal mania] to define a form of murderous madness without delirium. The aim, in conformity with article 64 of the penal code, introduced in 1810, was to save criminals from the guillotine in order to cure them.[33]

Esquirol and his pupils waged a fight against the death penalty, which contributed to the birth of medicolegal psychiatry. But this dispute among specialists also had a scientific aspect. It revealed what a battering the psychophysiological model originating in the Enlightenment took in the psychiatric knowledge of the first half of the nineteenth century. Two schools of thought, both hostile to ultra-Catholicism, clashed between 1810 and 1838: that of the physiologists and that of the doctrinaires. The first maintained a psychophysiological stance, and thus a monist conception of the unity of mental life as dominated by the physical organization. Represented by Broussais, Gall, Esquirol, and Auguste Comte, this school presented itself as progressive and atheist. The second, spiritualist and psychological, was more conservative and aimed to restore the double authority of the state and religion, while favoring economic liberalism. Personified in Théodore Jouffroy and Victor Cousin, it was inspired by German philosophy—Kant and Hegel—in affirming that the mind is an autonomous reality independent of the physical world and requiring to be explored from within, by introspection.

After repeated clashes, the two schools ended by adopting a middling position that resulted in the passing of the law of 1838. To the great satisfaction of the physiological psychiatrists, the madperson thus escaped the judicial system; while the doctrinaires could take pride in the fact that the creation of state asylums made it possible to combat social disorder and to correct what primary schooling, instituted in 1833, did not succeed in preventing.

Stripped of the ordinary rights of the citizen, the Esquirolian madman of 1838 bore no resemblance to the *aliéné* of Pinel's era. Separated now from his family, isolated and locked up for life, he was subjected to the control of a secularized psychiatric power. To intern and isolate: these were now the two visages of consolation and classification. The reign of this new mental medicine began with the death of Esquirol and lasted until around 1960, when the asylum age drew to a close as pharmaceuticals came into general use, replacing the tangible straitjacket with a chemical one.

As for Jean-Martin Charcot, the heir of the physiologists, he incorporated hysteria into psychiatric knowledge and made this neurosis, this "semimadness," into the paradigm of a new fin-de-siècle illness destined to invade the bodies of women and sow unease in masculine identity. Out of the encounter between Charcot and Freud came psychoanalysis, the new interpretive model of behavior for the twentieth century.

In studying the origins of a model of psychiatric knowledge that entered its terminal phase just as Foucault was beginning to tread the pathways of night, and seven years after Louis Althusser had experienced its last manifestations,[34] Jan Goldstein offered some thoughts on the future. Indeed the parallelism with the past is striking: The *querelles* of the nineteenth century are recurring today in the fierce debates between those who support genetic causality and psychopharmacology on one side, and the partisans of psychical causality on the other, in a context no longer dominated by monomania or hysteria, but rather by depression—the ultimate form of the malaise of Western culture at the dawn of the new millennium.

Like all bold thinkers—especially the ones who never gave in to normalization—Foucault was hated. As much as Sartre and Derrida, as much as Althusser and Deleuze. In France he was accused of being nihilistic, antidemocratic, and Heideggerian, in other words of having been a Nazi, since Heidegger had been one. Later he was rebuked for having supported the regime of the ayatollahs because he had been fascinated, in the streets of Teheran, by the uprising of a people who were revolting against their monarch in the name of a saint and because he had tried to understand the spiritual significance of a new kind of revolution,[35] and the unconditional support that one ought, or ought not, to give to the singularity of such an uprising.

In the United States, where his work was studied in many universities,[36] Foucault was often seen as a spell-binding destroyer of civilized morality. Not only had he undertaken to defend homosexuals at a time when they were still considered perverts and were punished by the law, but he had discovered a new experience of sexuality in the bars and saunas of California. The practice of S and M, he was saying in essence, is a creation and thus a subculture, a new way of utilizing the body as a source of pleasure. And he would include drugs in that, as long as their consumption did not result in alienation.

Since Foucault had taken not only to uttering such opinions, seen as subversive, but to wearing black leather jackets, it was not long before he was being regarded as mentally ill. Later he was portrayed retroactively as some sort of murderer because he had never practiced safe sex.[37] His accusers neglected to note that while there was general awareness of AIDS as a disease between 1981 and 1984, the degree of risk it entailed and its modes of transmission had not yet been clearly established.[38] There were many in the homosexual community, the one most affected, who still denied its existence. Foucault only realized at a very late stage that he had been contaminated, as we now know. "I think I've caught AIDS," he said to Georges Dumézil a few months before his death.[39]

Nine years later, the author of *History of Madness* was transformed by James Miller, a professor at the New School for Social Research in New York, into a "pathological case." In his book *The Passion of Michel Foucault*,[40] Miller resorted to the psychobiographic method inspired by the new conditioning therapies—themselves grounded in the violation of conscience—in order to reconstruct what he took to be the mental universe of the philosopher and to appraise in minute detail the demons that supposedly haunted his psyche.[41] Convinced that Foucault had deliberately contracted AIDS so as to fulfill his death wish, Miller concluded that the entire Foucauldian oeuvre was pervaded by a mystique of suicide, the origin of which went back, according to him, to three so-called traumatic memories recorded by the writer Hervé Guibert as the philosopher lay dying in the hospital of La Salpêtrière.[42]

The first of the "terrible dioramas" reported by Guibert showed the philosopher in childhood being taken by his father, who was a surgeon, into an operating room in the hospital in Poitiers where a man was having a limb amputated. In the second of these confidences, Foucault recalled the famous *séquestrée de Poitiers*, a woman discovered in 1901 to have been locked up by her family for many years, and emphasized how, upon seeing the inner courtyard where she had been confined, he had as a child felt a terror that later gave him a taste for tabloid sensationalism. Finally, the last of the memories reported by Guibert had to do with the presence at Foucault's high school during the German occupation of a number of students from Paris: they were more gifted than him and this made him feel threatened. He had cursed and hated them, and then seen them disappear into the maw of the final solution.

According to Miller, Foucault's father so humiliated him by forcing him to watch an amputation that Foucault lost his virility and remained fascinated all his life by the opening up of cadavers and the sight of torture. Likewise the sight of the mattress on which the sequestered woman of Poitiers had lain had given him a taste for enclosed spaces, labyrinths, and incarceration. As for his feelings of jealousy toward the Jewish students exterminated by the Nazis, it lay, according to Miller, at the root of Foucault's conviction that fascism had to be opposed, not just as a historical phenomenon, but as the power that determines, without our knowing it, our most routine actions. In any case, these three repressed traumatic experiences guided Foucault, on Miller's showing, down the tortuous pathways of a death cult—the sole explanation of his suicidal passion and his "desire" to contract AIDS.

One is left speechless at the stupidity of this putatively Freudian interpretation of the work and life of Michel Foucault, resting on nothing but extravagant hypotheses and reaching the most banal conclusion possible: Every book originates in the lived experience of its author.

A Nazi, a nihilist, an antidemocrat, and an Islamist for his French de-tractors; a great sadomasochistic contaminator and pathological case for certain of his American commentators (haunted to the point of delirium by their own personal sexual obsessions), the author of *History of Madness* had become, ten years after his death, one of the most widely read and admired French philosophers throughout the world, including in France itself, but at the cost of being considered also as the most infa-mous and perverse thinker of the second half of the century.[43]

The critique of *History of Madness* advanced by Jacques Derrida took the Foucauldian reversal as its point of departure. But Derrida was not interested in listing Foucault's "mistakes" or accusing him of nihilism. Not only did he defend the critical character of Foucault's discourse, he asserted the necessity for any critical discourse to acknowledge its debt to the object critiqued and emphasized that the conscience of the disciple, when it engages in dialogue with that of the master, is always an unhappy conscience. Derrida did not wait long to speak his piece, doing so in a lecture on the theme "*cogito* and history of madness" given on 3 March 1963 at the Collège de Philosophie.[44]

His polemic bore on the status of the Cartesian *cogito* with respect to the history of madness. Foucault made a distinction in Descartes be-tween the exercise of madness and the activity of dreaming. He empha-sized that Descartes had excluded madness from the *cogito*, and that this decree of exclusion in a sense heralded the political decision to carry out the *grande renfermement* (1656). On the contrary—and still according to Foucault—dreaming in the Cartesian sense was one of the virtualities of the subject; it was the influence of the *malin genie* [evil genius] that caused its sensible images to become deceptive.

Just as Henri Gouhier had refused to see the famous phrase from the *Meditations*, "*Mais quoi! ce sont des fous*," as an expression of ostracism against madness, Derrida likewise refused Foucault the right to perform an act of confinement on the *cogito*.

Where Foucault represented Descartes as saying "man may well be mad if the *cogito* is not," Derrida replied that, with the act of the *cogito*, thought no longer needed to fear madness, because "the *cogito* holds good even if I am mad." Consequently, in Descartes, madness is included in the *cogito*, said Derrida, and its fissure is internal to reason. As for the evil genius, the hypothesis was only discarded by Descartes—still according to Derrida—the better to highlight the fact that the *cogito* would remain true, even if "craziness" [*affolement*] prevailed everywhere. So Derrida was accusing Foucault of constituting an event as structure: the ostracism against madness began not with the *cogito* but with the victory of Socrates over the pre-Socratics. In order to think the history of madness outside the bounds of a structural totality always threatening to turn totalitarian, it was necessary to show that the division between reason and madness existed in the history of philosophy as an original presence amply overspilling the system in which Foucault had inscribed it.

Derrida was not therefore taking aim at Foucault's construction of a domain of madness absent from the archives but at an interpretation he deemed too restrictive, because too structural, of the system of divisions. This was the first stage of a critique internal to the history of French structuralism.[45] With it Derrida was proposing, as Deleuze was to do along other lines, to deconstruct the overly dogmatic utilization of the data of Saussurian linguistics in the so-called human sciences. In terms of historiography, Derrida was tending toward the thesis later associated with Ellenberger: madness exists prior to the gesture of the French classic age, constituting it as the Other of reason. For Derrida the exclusion is prior to the *cogito* and goes back to Socrates; for Ellenberger madness is a fact of culture.

Foucault was present in the hall when Derrida delivered his lecture on 3 March 1963. He kept silent. When Derrida's *Writing and Difference*, which includes the lecture, was published, he even sent Derrida a warmly worded letter. The dispute broke out subsequently, with Foucault composing a two-part reply to Derrida, which he included in the 1972 edition of *History of Madness*. "Sorry to get back to you so late," he said to Derrida in his dedication. The first part consisted of a long philosophical discussion of the status of the *cogito*, the second was a terrible ad hominem attack on Derrida's whole approach, reduced by Foucault to "textualization" and "small-time pedagogy."

The two men did not meet for nine years. In 1981, when Derrida was giving a seminar in Prague with dissident intellectuals, he was arrested and accused of drug trafficking. From Paris, Foucault was quick to support him and launch an appeal in his favor on the radio.[46] In the tempest of this struggle for freedom, the philosopher of the pathways of night was reconciled with the philosopher of deconstruction at just the time when *History of Madness* was being stigmatized by its detractors as a monument of antidemocracy.[47]

I never met Michel Foucault, whose work I discovered upon reading *Words and Things* in the summer of 1966.[48] This dazzling book, written with knife-edged incisiveness in the manner of a great novel of initiation, posed an essential question to the generation to which I belonged, the post-Sartrean generation if you like: How were we to move on from the philosophy of commitment without reverting to the monotony of phantasmal life or of just managing the business of living?

Compared to *Mein Kampf* by an unhinged psychoanalyst,[49] then violently criticized by those who blamed Foucault for undermining the rights of man and for not being "democratic" enough, this work reopened the great question of humanism posed by Sartre after the liberation, in his controversy with Heidegger.

On 28 October 1945 Sartre gave his famous public lecture "Existentialism Is a Humanism,"[50] in which he popularized his theory of freedom grounded in theses laid down in *Being and Nothingness*. After this flourish he opened the columns of *Les Temps Modernes* to a debate on Heidegger's engagement with Nazism.[51] The question addressed by all the participants was this: Was Heidegger's stance imputable to fleeting error, or was it the logical outcome of a philosophical orientation that, in promoting the reconnection of man with his own roots, had ended by finding in Nazism the doctrine of salvation that matched the criteria it had set? Some maintained that Heidegger's commitment was no more than an accident that did not impinge on the essential portion of his work as a philosopher, while others asserted on the contrary that this commitment had its roots in a ground identical to that from which Nazism had sprung.

Heidegger, it is well known, had been one of the great promoters, especially within the universities, of "working toward the Führer."[52] After World War Two his strongest supporter had been the French philosopher

Jean Beaufret, a former member of the Resistance against the Nazi occupation, and this had enabled him to conceal the extent of his support of Nazism. Thanks to Beaufret, the fact that the question of Heidegger's engagement was still an unresolved issue was forgotten in France for many years. For it is in fact impossible to deny the extent of the attachment of Heidegger's philosophy to Nazism; just as it is impossible to reduce his thought to the simple dimensions of a handbook for SS officers.[53]

It remains the case that in his *Letter on Humanism* Heidegger had portrayed every form of humanism—and existentialism in particular—as a new metaphysics for a modern mankind submerged in the lethargy of an existence conditioned by technology and the illusions of progress.[54]

The antihumanism of which Foucault (and for that matter Louis Althusser) was accused was different in kind, even if the polemic centered on him in France was a continuation of the debate that had begun with the *querelle* between Sartre and Heidegger. If the most advanced civilization in Europe, so the argument ran, was capable of putting into operation at Auschwitz hitherto unequalled powers of destruction and self-destruction, that meant that inhumanity—the death wish, in other words—lay at the heart of the human and not outside it, in the depths of some improbable animality.

Consequently the humanist discourse bore within itself the seeds of a possible annihilation of its own values. In the words of Claude Lévi-Strauss: "In seeing mankind apart from the rest of creation, in a different perspective, western humanism deprived it of a protective glacis. When man knows no further limit to his power, he goes on to destroy himself. Consider the death camps, and, on a different plane, but with tragic consequences this time for the whole of humanity, pollution."[55]

For Foucault, as for Derrida and Deleuze, it was imperative to continually question such ideals as the rights of man, humanism, and democracy, so as to uncover, at the very core of that which presents itself as the most refined expression of Western culture, the traces of a dark force—or sometimes just the traces of that little everyday, nondescript fascism—that never ceases to threaten their fragile equilibrium.[56]

In *Words and Things* Foucault deployed a dazzling erudition. As for his central thesis, it supplied a way to think the question of human destiny in a world in which mankind has become, thanks to progress in the life sciences, both an object of knowledge and the murderer of itself. With this critique of humanism Foucault revived the stance of the Frankfurt school against Heidegger's thought: the invention of a form of critical thought capable not only of analyzing the mechanisms of power at work in industrial societies but also of generating ways of resisting the biologization of the mind, without succumbing either to resignation or to a simplistic humanism grounded in good conscience and rationality.

Like Theodor Adorno and Max Horkheimer, who had also posed questions regarding the limits of reason, but with different gestures, Foucault sought to trouble the order of the world, to force its obscure part, its disorder, its heterogeneity to well up out of the apparent sovereignty of order.[57] He took part resolutely in the conceptual adventure, making the conceptuality proper to the human sciences an object of passion upon which an entire generation, formed in the secularized and republican university system, was invited to reflect in critical fashion. In modeling themselves upon the life sciences, he said, the human sciences risked reducing man to an object and perhaps destroying him. From this perspective, *Words and Things* was the logical successor to *History of Madness*: "The history of madness would be the history of the Other, of that which is both internal and foreign to a culture, and thus to be excluded (to counter the internal threat), but by confining it (to reduce its alterity). The history of the order of things would be the history of the Same—of that which, for a culture, is both dispersed and kindred, and so to be distinguished by marks and gathered into identities."[58]

From this perspective, Foucault accorded a privileged status to psychoanalysis, linguistics, and ethnology: they dissolved the notion of man, he said, without pretending to reconstitute man as an observable positivistic datum. This was the deep meaning of the last lines of the work, which were understood, notably by Sartre but by many others too, as a reactionary manifesto hostile to any form of humanism and existential commitment: "So one can wager that man would be wiped away, like a face in the sand at the edge of the sea."[59]

Against Sartre, whom he forgave neither his attitude during the occupation nor his philosophy of the subject, Georges Canguilhem undertook to defend Foucault vigorously then, recalling, as he so often did, that Jean Cavaillès had "refused in advance, by participating in the history he lived out tragically right up to death, the argument of those who try to discredit structuralism by claiming it can only engender, among other misdeeds, passivity in the face of the fait accompli."[60]

The homage thus offered to the philosopher of the pathways of night, by the former Resistance fighter who had become France's great master of the history of science, signified clearly that Foucault's passionate commitment to conceptuality was one of the most fecund ways for the intellectual generation of the 1960s to reacquire the taste for heroism in thought.

4. LOUIS ALTHUSSER

{THE MURDER SCENE}

A LFRED HITCHCOCK SHOT MURDER SCENES LIKE LOVE
scenes and love scenes like murder scenes. In each of his films,
with ferocious skill, the master of suspense places the viewer in a trou-
bling situation, sometimes making him the author of a crime of which he
is no more than the virtual witness, sometimes the central character in a
carnal relationship in which, by definition, she can never participate. As
for Hitchcock's heroes, whether killers or victims, Prince Charmings or
Cinderellas, spies or assassins, they are always prey to a sort of logic of
surrender to impulse that makes them strangers to themselves and strips
them of any psychological consistency. A filmmaker of the unconscious,
of repression and fetishism, Hitchcock filmed dreams as reality and desire as perversion: between the sublime and the abject.

No doubt it may be thought scandalous at first to compare the
autobiography of Louis Althusser, *The Future Lasts a Long Time*,[1] to a
Hitchcock narrative. And yet in reading Althusser's work, you get an
impression of disturbing strangeness as strong as the one you get from
seeing *North by Northwest*, *Psycho*, or *Marnie*.

It was in 1985 that the philosopher decided to compose a written account of the scene of the murder of his wife, Hélène Rytmann,[2] after reading the account by Claude Sarraute, a journalist with *Le Monde*, of Issei Sagawa, a Japanese criminal who killed a young Dutch woman in Paris, then dismembered and ate her body. Diagnosed as not responsible for his actions at the time of the deed, and therefore mentally unfit to stand trial under article 64 of the French penal code,[3] he was given psychiatric treatment and then returned to Japan, where, bizarrely, he was discharged and declared "normal," meaning responsible for his actions. But instead of being tried there, as the unhappy parents of the victim were demanding, he kept his freedom and even had a career as an actor in pornographic films and best-selling author. He said about his crime that the young woman did not suffer when he killed her and that anthropophagy was an act of love. Sagawa subsequently came to be regarded as a real expert in criminal matters and was frequently sought out by the press for authoritative commentary whenever a murder was committed.

In her article Claude Sarraute perfidiously made a connection between Sagawa's case and Althusser's. "We in the media," she said, "as soon as we spot a prestigious name mixed up in a juicy trial, like Althusser or Thibault d'Orléans, make a meal out of it. The victim? She doesn't earn three lines. The star is the perpetrator."[4]

The author of this malicious text made the point, quite correctly and without even realizing it herself, that in major criminal trials the perpetrator is necessarily the hero, since he is called upon to account for his actions before the court and the victims. A perpetrator who escaped the justice system without having been recognized as mad could never be a hero. Thus in societies where a code of civil rights exists, a criminal has the choice between an impunity that condemns him to perpetual anonymity, to an abject life of flight and cowardice, and a confrontation with the law that makes him the author of his own deed, that is to say, a subject of rights. It is at this cost, and only at this cost, that even the worst of criminals can reconcile himself with his own destiny.

In this respect, Claude Sarraute was blind to the utter dissimilarity between the Sagawa case and that of Louis Althusser. Recognized as irresponsible, Sagawa nonetheless remained guilty of a murderous act for which he was constrained to undergo psychiatric confinement and treatment. He had thus become, in the eyes of French law, guilty of but not responsible for his actions, in other words a subject recognized as mentally ill. But upon returning to his own country, where he ought to have continued to be treated as such, he was recognized as responsible for his actions and then released without ever being tried—which is a real aberration. He thus became not the hero of a criminal act following which he ought logically to have met his fate through being found guilty and incarcerated, but a personality at once guilty, not responsible, responsible, and perverted. Guilty and not responsible for a crime that remained unpunished; responsible for the same crime according to the attitude of his Japanese judges, who by declaring him "normal" authorized him to become a media personality; and a pervert because elevated de facto by public opinion to the status of expert in criminology. Recognized as mad, Sagawa could escape trial, but once declared sane, he should have been tried.

In this affair the Japanese justice system therefore brought upon itself the guilt of a real crime by authorizing a murderer not only to escape any legal sanction but also to transform his deed into psychiatric credentials.

One sees why Althusser was appalled at being mentioned in connection with this affair, and I can bear direct witness to the suffering it caused him. Sarraute had dared to compare him to a criminal who had succeeded in evading human justice while making a mockery of it and whose fate was radically different to his own. Of course, the Japanese cannibal and the French philosopher had both been set free. But the former, once acknowledged as "normal," was able to turn the gravity of his deed to derision by depicting it as a monstrous testimony of love, whereas the latter, designated mentally ill by experts, had never had the chance to revendicate full psychical and juridical responsibility for an act for which he had confessed he was, and indeed felt himself to be, guilty. What Louis Althusser was suffering from in 1985 was having been robbed of his own deed and deprived of a trial, by virtue of a law proclaiming that "there is neither crime nor delict when the person suspected was in a state of dementia at the time of the deed."

Introduced into the penal code in 1810 and confirmed repeatedly since 1838 despite numerous attempts at reform, article 64, which was finally changed in 1992, made it possible for criminals assessed as insane to escape the death penalty. And that had marked an important step in the long history of the campaign to abolish the death penalty, just as the great alienists in the tradition of Esquirol had intended it should.

In November 1980, when Louis Althusser strangled his wife, the death penalty had not yet been abolished in France. Despite that, article 64 was already obsolete, and was denounced as such, because it deprived the accused of any right to be heard, regardless of what he had to say.

In other words, by this article every accused person assessed as being mad could still be designated not responsible for an act that he had nevertheless committed—but which was juridically rendered null—and then be judged unpunishable because in juridical terms his action did not exist. So he automatically got the benefit of a declaration that there were no grounds for proceeding against him, which not only effaced the story of his crime from the memory of man but also made him a non-subject of rights, one of the "disappeared":[5] "For the average reader, for whom certain newspapers cater without ever distinguishing between *folie* [madness] as an acute but passing state, and *maladie mentale* [mental illness], which is a destiny, the *fou* [madperson] is straightaway held to be 'mentally ill,' with the emphasis falling on 'ill,' and consequently fit to be locked up, and locked up for life: *Lebenstod*, as the German press puts it so well."[6]

For twelve years this murder scene, which took place at dawn on 17 November 1980 in an apartment in the École Normale Supérieure (ENS) in the rue d'Ulm and which had long been laid at the feet of the philosopher, was neither known, nor explained, nor recounted, nor even interpreted. No one ever knew, before the posthumous publication of *The Future Lasts a Long Time* in 1992, how the surrender to impulse had taken place. Filed away in the archives of the hospital administration, the murder scene had thus been, so to speak, annihilated, effaced, forgotten, and repressed, while its author, once celebrated or hated throughout the world, lived out a spectral existence.

The only things made known to the press and the public were the conclusions of the autopsy and the psychiatric assessment. Thus it was on record that Hélène Rytmann died as a result of strangulation with fracture of the larynx and rupture of the two thyroid cords but with no visible external signs. And subsequently it became known that three psychiatric experts (Serge Brion, Alain Diederichs, and Roger Ropert) had recommended application of article 64, on the grounds that "wife-murder by manual strangulation was committed without any additional violence, in the course of [an] iatrogenic hallucinatory episode complicated by melancholic depression."

Most journalists in the intellectual press avoided such technicalities, soberly pointing out that the philosopher suffered from manic-depressive psychosis and that he had strangled his wife in the course of an acute crisis of melancholy, without even realizing it.[7] Some of them, though, were quick to exploit this tragedy by waging a campaign against what, in their eyes, symbolized not only a genuine ignominy but a real menace to civilization.

Certainly none descended to the level of the reporter for the newspaper *Minute*, who triumphantly wrote that "the 'abnormal superior' represents all by himself a striking summary of communism . . . which began in the mists of philosophy and ended up in a sordid Grand Guignol. . . . He ought to have been barred from teaching, except that he was untouchable, precisely because he was a communist."[8]

With apparently greater subtlety but in a much more perverse fashion, Dominique Jamet imagined a "conspiracy" woven by the French Communist Party and certain intellectuals in order to spare the "assassin" Louis Althusser the nuisance of being questioned by the police. His message was basically that the furious champions of equality had succeeded in reestablishing privileges worthy of the old aristocracy in France:

> The assassin isn't just a nobody, isn't just the first person to happen along, isn't just anybody at all. A former student at the École Normale Supérieure, the site of the crime, of which he became the secretary general, a renowned theorist of Marxism, an eminent member of the Communist party, the author of a number of authoritative works, he is also an eminent member of the French intellectual establishment. He has the powerful on his side. . . . And so friends of his, physicians, officials in charge, all organize a con-

spiracy around the philosopher for the purpose of steering him clear of the bother, the torment, and the humiliation that await those of his ilk. . . . They put him in a car, they whisk him away from the very soft, very slow police; they would have kept him out of the papers if they could, and they nearly did. . . . You would think that nothing had changed since the epoch when the duc de Choiseul-Praslin murdered his wife, except for the fact that the intellectuals have now swollen the ranks of those aristocrats whose noble heads you never, except in periods of revolution, see hanging from any lamppost.[9]

Among the intellectuals implicitly pointed to by Dominique Jamet as conspirators and accomplices of a communist plot were Régis Debray, Étienne Balibar, and Jacques Derrida, who were the first to take steps, along with Dr. Pierre Étienne and Jean Bousquet,[10] to have Althusser placed in the Saint-Anne hospital. It is certainly true that, with due regard for his past, the philosopher was interned directly in a psychiatric facility without first undergoing detention at a police station. He did not have to remain naked for twenty-four hours in a holding cell furnished only with a mattress on the floor. And he did not have to submit to formal interrogation, on account of the simple fact that he had confessed to the murder, and that he alone, in the circumstances, could have committed it.

This was the "privilege" from which he benefited, to the great fury of Roger Peyrefitte, the minister of justice and a former student at the ENS, who would have preferred that they treat him, against psychiatric advice, as an ordinary criminal, indeed as a killer unprotected by article 64. No doubt the minister, just like the journalist, was ignorant of how much Louis Althusser himself would have preferred to answer for his deed before a jury in a criminal court, even at the risk of the death sentence, sooner than be dispossessed by psychiatric experts of his word, his history, and his gesture.

In reality this populist and revanchist discourse, antielitist and antiintellectual—which was springing up everywhere at this time and has continued to grow in volume ever since[11]—signified that in the eyes of a section of public opinion dominated by hatred of defiant consciences, the murder committed by Althusser had to be merely the visible part of a much more dreadful crime: the one perpetrated for decades by all the communists in every country in the world, who were evidently responsible for the crimes of Stalinism and totally guilty of concealing them in the name of a revolutionary ideal whose sole aim had been to snuff out democratic freedoms.

Labeled the last great thinker of Marxism, Althusser was portrayed as one who, from inside a party considered detestable, had imparted a taste for revolutionary commitment grounded in conceptual philosophy to the intellectual elite of the rue d'Ulm between 1960 and 1975. Worse in the eyes of his detractors, Althusser had inscribed both Marxism and communism in the history of philosophy.[12] Thus he was considered a criminal three times over: because he had legitimated philosophically a current of thought judged responsible for the Gulag; because after having criticized Stalinism he had dared to see in the Chinese Cultural Revolution an event with the capacity to subvert both bourgeois society and Stalinist socialism;[13] and finally because he had, it was said, perverted the elite of French youth by introducing the cult of a criminal ideology into the heart of one of the finest institutions of the French Republic. It was no wonder that such a disastrous adventure had been orchestrated by a mentally ill individual and had concluded with a murderous act.

The message being broadcast after November 1980 was that it was time to forget Althusser, forget his homicidal philosophy,[14] forget the act that led him into the hell of unreason—the implicit corollary being that we ought also to forget or repress everything the philosopher's teaching had given to a generation marked by the anticolonialist commitment of Sartre, a generation that had gone on to seek, in a rigorously rethought Marxism, something other than pure and simple adhesion to Soviet socialism, which everyone knew and admitted had ended by producing the Gulag.

Like Sartre, Althusser had in effect been able to think against himself, that is, against the real socialism to which he had made his commitment, for better or worse, upon emerging from a Catholic upbringing. He did, admittedly, persist in inscribing texts by Lenin and Mao Zedong in the tradition of philosophical conceptuality to which belonged names like Canguilhem, Gaston Bachelard, Spinoza, Hegel, Montesquieu, and Freud; and there may indeed be errant, ridiculous, or scandalous aspects to that.

But that was the price to be paid, you might say, for attempting to demonstrate that there could be more to Marxism than the simple repetition of dogmas rehearsed ad infinitum by the communist parties. Something different to the Nazism to which its critics endlessly compared it, forgetting that the two totalitarian systems had different origins, different projects, and different organizational structures. Stalinism was the outcome of the twisting awry of an ideal of progress and equality (communism), while Nazism was no more than the putting into operation of a genocidal intention grounded in the cult of race and blood. I might point out, in this regard, that the twisting of an ideal into its contrary is always infinitely graver, and harder to combat, than the straightforward execution of a project that never had any goal but mass murder from the start. For such twisting awry not only destroys the bodies of human beings, it inflicts injury on the human dream and the human imaginary. From that point of view, you could even say that the Gulag was worse than the Shoah.

Althusser advocated the autonomy of Marxist theory, which he wanted to make into a science of politics articulated around the principle of dialectical materialism. Hence he made a distinction between this theory and a philosophy of consciousness grounded in the subject. A philosopher of Marxism rather than a Marxist philosopher, he emphasized that revolutionary praxis, and thus subjective commitment, were irreducible to consciousness of self. Hence his critique of classic humanism. And hence his valorization of "theoretical antihumanism" and a conception of history as "a process without subject or end." Like Canguilhem and Foucault, and despite subscribing to a theory of the Freudian unconscious revisited by Lacan, he attacked all forms of behavioral psychology, insisting that political praxis only made sense if it was the expression of a conceptual philosophy capable of detaching itself from speculative metaphysics and becoming, through combat, an instrument of the class struggle in the realm of theory.

So without ever having been a Heideggerian in the strict sense, having in fact rejected the approach of Jean Beaufret, Althusser drew upon concepts from the *Letter on Humanism* to oppose Sartrean existentialism. Through theoretical antihumanism and a refusal to let subjectivity intrude into history, he wished to exclude any form of lived psychological experience from political commitment and to demonstrate once more the superiority in this domain of conceptual philosophy over the philosophy of consciousness. At the risk, as we shall see, of suppressing the very notion of the subject, of smothering it in a logical structure of a totalitarian kind.

Through his friend Jacques Martin, a philosopher and ENS graduate, Althusser had discovered the oeuvres of Cavaillès and Canguilhem, which impelled him to propose his own reading of the oeuvre of Marx and so combine conceptual philosophy and a philosophy of commitment. It was also through Martin that he had become acquainted with Foucault, whose studies at the ENS he influenced, and with whom he forged a bond based on a common interest in the history of madness. And finally it was to Jacques Martin, whom he was unable to prevent from dying by his own hand, that he dedicated his *Pour Marx*: "He, a suffering but warm-hearted homosexual, became an incomparable friend in the distance of his latent schizophrenia. . . . Michel Foucault loved him as much as I did."[15]

When he came to know *History of Madness*, and later *Birth of the Clinic*, Althusser perceived that a true seam of thought lay embedded in the texture of these two dazzling books and knew that he wanted to mine it for concepts that he could put to use to make Marxism into a theory of history. As well, he found a style of cogitation in the crepuscular language of the philosopher that obliged him to confront philosophically the reality of his own melancholy, the reality that constantly escaped him, making him one of the shipwrecked ones of reason. For the future philosopher of Marxism was first and foremost a melancholic philosopher, a philosopher whose melancholy had been debaptized, concealed beneath other maladies,[16] and even stripped of its name by the discourse of psychiatry. In September 1962 he wrote to Franca Madonia: "Finished reading this book . . . stunning, astonishing, a work of genius, an excavation and simultaneously a radiance full of views and flashes of lightning, patches of night and shafts of dawn, this book crepuscular like Nietzsche but luminous as an equation."[17] During the academic year 1962–63 Althusser organized a seminar for the students of the ENS dedicated to structuralism, in which he himself spoke on *History of Madness*.[18]

Confinement was something Althusser had experienced long before entering the infernal cycle of psychiatric internment. Having been a student in Jean Guitton's *khâgne* in Lyon, Althusser should have entered the ENS in 1939, at the age of twenty-one. Instead he was called up to serve as a student officer on the banks of the Loire, then evacuated toward Vannes, and finally captured by the German army. Althusser spent the next five years in captivity, in Stalag XA, near Schleswig, without ever having chosen the slightest commitment. At the conclusion of a war of which he had known only the most absurd and frozen aspect but that had been so decisive for the philosophical generation to which he belonged, Althusser was thus already the prisoner of an inner turmoil, untouched by glory and heroism but equally untouched by any suspicion of collaboration with the enemy.[19] It was in the depth of this captivity, experienced as humiliation and punctuated by melancholic episodes, that he renounced the integrist and royalist Catholicism he had grown up with, and joined the French Communist Party, the party of those who had faced firing squads: "It was in prison camp that I first heard Marxism discussed by a Parisian lawyer in transit—and that I actually met a communist, a single one."[20]

In the 1960s Althusser really set about strengthening the theory of the communist movement, and that is why, soon after publication, his two major works—*For Marx* and *To Read "Capital"*[21]—were translated into many languages. Flanked by his ENS students, the philosopher of Marxism became, for the militants of the international communist movement, a new Marx, with a messianic destiny, not just another political leader mechanically reciting dogmas and slogans. The man of the rue d'Ulm had assigned himself the task, through a teaching both rigorous and collective, of awakening the soul of the world.

But because this great appeal to the revolt of consciences was launched at a moment when communism was already falling prey to an internal process of decomposition, Althusser's message appeared to be self-condemned either to regress into flamboyant theorizing or to amount to no more than the finale of a prolonged melancholy lamentation. So there was something both incandescent and transitory about it, as if, before even having had the chance to be incarnated in the course of history or the time to create a legacy for the future, it had already been gripped by the silence of memory and the vacuity of death.

It is a commonplace that all the great philosophical systems of the nineteenth century were constructed like Greek tragedies, because they all issued from the great theater of the Revolution of 1789. Napoleon said to Goethe in 1808 that politics would be the destiny of European man in the future; that meant that the essence of tragedy would no longer be the confrontation between men and gods but the action by which mankind itself, the successor of gods and kings, would take its own history, and that of the peoples, into its own hands.

Heir to these systems, whose dogmas he wished to overcome, Althusser had tried to think the communism of the second half of the twentieth century as the possible reactualization of revolutionary heroism, with philosophy as its new great theater, a theater of the body, of the unconscious, and of excess, a theater of the real and of movement. To become that, it would have to be capable of "renouncing its ideological reveries and moving on to the study of reality itself."[22] Jacques Derrida wrote: "What I love most in him, doubtless because it was him, that which fascinated me in him and which others no doubt knew better and at much closer range than me, were his feeling and taste for grandeur, for a certain grandeur, for the great theater of political tragedy in which excess engages, misdirects, or breaks without pity the private bodies of its actors."[23]

This sense of theatricality was, for Althusser, a way of renewing the gesture of Karl Marx, the gesture with which, in drafting the *Economic and Philosophical Manuscripts of 1844* and in reading the works of Ludwig Feuerbach, the future theorist of capitalism had broken away from Hegelian philosophy, moving from an abstract conception of the movement of history to revolutionary commitment. Philosophers, Marx said, "have hitherto merely interpreted the world; it is a question of transforming it."[24]

After the completion of the judicial investigation of Althusser's case, Judge Guy Joly decided that there were no grounds to proceed. A warrant of confinement was subsequently issued by the Paris police prefecture, and with that Louis Althusser lost all the rights of a citizen. The ENS then mandated his retirement and requested his family and friends to clear out the apartment he had occupied ever since his return from prison camp, on the ground floor at the southwest corner of the main building, facing the infirmary in which his friend Dr. Pierre Étienne lived. In June 1980 Althusser left the Saint-Anne hospital for the Eau Vive clinic at Soisy-sur-Seine, which he knew well, and in July 1983 he took up residence in an apartment in rue Lucien Leuwen in Paris.

For ten years, between the date of the murder and that of his death on 22 October 1990, Louis Althusser lived a strange life as a specter, a dead man walking, a man who had become his own other—the sinister hero of a crime assessed, autopsied, reduced to the prose of a jargon-filled report—without even having access to the psychiatric meaning of his deed, but who had not yet passed through the portals of the kingdom of shadows: the negative and tragic image of the concept of "trial-without-a-subject" that he himself had forged to define the place of subjectivity in history.

For that matter the very history of communism mimicked the disaster that had shattered his life. A mute spectator, he took in the implosion of the Soviet Union, the dismantling of its empire, and the slow erosion of institutions that had, for sixty years and despite the crimes of Stalinism, succeeded in offering an ideal of dignity, a utopia, a dream, a faith, and also a culture, to the working classes of the democratic countries. In these circumstances neither Marxism nor the parties that had tried to realize these ideals appeared to have any future.

After the publication of Claude Sarraute's article, the one that paired Althusser with the Japanese cannibal, he began to dream of "reappearing on the public stage."[25] But he knew that, to accomplish such a return, he would have to confront the deed that had made him into a murderer without name or voice. He would have to proceed, in narrative, with the trial that had never taken place. He would have to set down in writing the terrible murder scene that he continually described to members of his inner circle, always in the same terms, always evoking the same memories, the same enigma: "I killed a woman who was everything to me during a crisis of mental confusion, she who loved me to the point of wanting only to die because she could not continue living. And no doubt in my confusion and unconsciousness I 'did her this service,' which she did not try to prevent, but from which she died."[26]

As long as this scene, a hundred times repeated, was not consigned to writing, the name of Althusser and the significance of his philosophical oeuvre would continue to be the object of a complete repression. So it had to be made public, this scene, in other words made into a work, for otherwise it would be endlessly reproduced, recounted, disseminated, falsified, interpreted, by countless witnesses or nonwitnesses who would have no hesitation, in the absence of any trace or archive, in standing in for the author of the crime and speaking in his place.

In 1983 Philippe Sollers was the first to appropriate the scene and describe the strangulation at length in the novel *Femmes*.[27] Comparing the madness of Lacan's last years to Althusser's, the narrator imagined by Sollers turned Althusser into an abject individual filled with hatred for women, especially with unconscious detestation for Hélène: "Small dry shape in a beret, older than him, like a governess. Extraordinarily antipathetic." She makes him quake with fear, because her intransigence—she had been a militant communist and anti-Nazi resister—torments him unremittingly, and in the end he strangles her, knowingly and in full awareness, with a scarf: "She was poisoning him . . . sucking the air out of him . . . asphyxiating him. . . . One night . . . since the time he had been thinking about it, surely. . . . He takes a scarf, he soundlessly approaches this sleeping woman to whom, all in all, he owes so much; this woman who put up with him, helped him, encouraged him, cared for him in his neurosis. . . . But who has also become, little by little, the grimacing mirror of his own defeat, his failure, his groundless culpability."[28] To this description of a strangulation duly premeditated by a murderous philosopher was appended the judgment of the narrator. The murder perpetrated by Lutz, he says, resembles in reverse the one depicted in Nagisa Oshima's 1976 film *In the Realm of the Senses*: "Where one sees the insatiable whore slowly strangle her consenting partner, sitting astride him, at the moment, indefinitely prolonged, of orgasm . . . and then castrate him."[29]

Two years after having been thus transformed into a sexual pervert right out of the psychiatric imagination of Krafft-Ebing, Althusser was converted by Jean Guitton into a mystic monk, more of a Catholic Pétainist than a communist graced by philosophy. In an interview published in autumn 1985, the academician recalled that the philosopher had been his *khâgne* student in 1938, that at that time he had wanted to become a Trappist, and finally that "his wife, who resembled Mother Teresa, was a pure mystic of communism." And he went on to say: "I sincerely think that he killed his wife out of love of her. It was a crime of mystical love. And is there such a great distance between a criminal and a saint? . . . It is not my business to defend him, but to aid him in the depth of his distress. . . . When I learned of the crime, I went to see him often at Saint-Anne, then I took steps to have him transferred to another establishment and . . . to have the justice system consider him a madman, not a criminal." Guitton then declared that he, like Althusser, had passed the whole of World War Two in captivity, that he was glad of it, that it was a captivity "accepted with great consent," and that he was proud to have remained, even today, "openly faithful to Marshal Pétain."[30]

In 1988 Régis Debray gave a rather sober account of the murder scene, comparing it to an altruistic suicide: "He suffocated her under a pillow to save her from the anguish that was suffocating him. A beautiful proof of love . . . that one can save one's skin while sacrificing oneself for the other, only to take upon oneself all the pain of living."[31]

By this time Althusser had already composed his autobiography. More than once he stated his desire to see it published, and he told certain members of his circle what it contained. But he never made up his mind to send it to a publisher, which obviously meant, contrary to what he said, that he preferred to continue to sojourn in the kingdom of the dead rather than reappear in the land of the living. That is why he wrote the murder scene as the posthumous preface to a tale from beyond the grave, through which a narrator tries to reconstruct for posterity the elements of an unusual story of inevitable disaster.[32] One might also hypothesize that, in thus recounting the arc of his life *from his death*, Althusser avoided having to deal with all the comment that it would certainly have provoked.

Speaking privately to André Malraux, Charles de Gaulle had set the Machiavellian notion of *fortuna*—the opportune moment, in the sense of the Greek work *kairos*—against the idea of the long term, emphasizing that in politics and in war one always had to be prepared to act at the right moment, on penalty of being hurled into the long duration of an eternal future, a future that lasts a long time [*un avenir qui dure longtemps*]. In choosing this phrase for the title of his book, Althusser was placing his narrative under the sign of eternal time, of the *longue durée* of death, if you like: the time of unfinished mourning, the time of melancholy. This was a way of saying that he had always been in mourning for himself, for his own death at the hands of his mother and wife, and that the composition of his autobiography might be able to open a radiant future to him, that of his looming plunge into the eternal time of death: "So then life can still, despite its dramas, be beautiful. I am sixty-seven, but I finally feel—I who had no youth, for I was not loved for myself—I feel younger than ever, even if the business must end soon. Yes, the future lasts a long time."[33] In either case, it is the murder scene that must remain the pure event, beyond life, beyond death, beyond even the infinite circle that erases the boundaries between the world of the living and the kingdom of the dead.

Rightly convinced, his denials notwithstanding, that his deed had definitively interrupted his engagement in theoretical pursuits, he preferred not to face, while still alive, a second burial that would have deprived him once again of any right to speak. And it was in writing this scene for posterity (not to redeem himself, while alive, for a responsibility he assumed outside the bounds of human justice), that he succeeded in punishing himself alone—like the hero of a tragedy—for the crime he had committed. An ultimate way to take his own philosophical destiny in hand.

In this respect, let me emphasize that, in order to attain its ontological significance and at the same time incarnate the reality of an act the truth of which had eluded all commentators, the murder scene could only be written once and uniquely by its author transformed into a narrator already dead. At this cost, and at this cost only, could it acquire the value of a true archive, meaning a trace, a proof, a witnessing capable of guaranteeing that the criminal act had indeed taken place and that he who was accused of it was indeed its author.

Just as I retain it in memory, full and precise down to the smallest details, engraved in me through all my suffering and forever—between two darknesses, the one which I was emerging from without knowing what it was, and the one into which I was going to enter, I am going to state the when and the how: here is the murder scene as I lived it. . . . Before me: Hélène lying on her back, also wearing a dressing gown. Her bedpan is lying on the edge of the bed, her legs are splayed on the carpet of the floor. Kneeling beside her, leaning over her body, I am engaged in massaging her neck. I have often had occasion to silently massage the nape of her neck, her upper back, and her lower back: I had learned the technique from a fellow prisoner, little Clerc, a professional football player and an expert in everything. But this time it is the front of her neck I am massaging. I press my two thumbs into the hollow of flesh that borders the top of the sternum, and, applying force, I slowly reach, one thumb toward the right, one thumb toward the left at an angle, the firmer area below the ears. I am massaging in a V. I feel enormous muscular fatigue in my forearms: I know, massaging always causes me discomfort. Hélène's face is immobile and serene, her open eyes are fixed on the ceiling. And suddenly I am struck with terror: her eyes are interminably fixed, and above all here is the tip of her tongue lying, unusually and peacefully, between her teeth and her lips. I had certainly seen corpses before, but I had never seen the face of a strangled woman in my life. And yet I know that this is a strangled woman. What is happening? I stand up and scream: I've strangled Hélène![34]

When one reads this scene one is struck immediately by the simplicity with which the narrator recounts the murder and how he becomes aware of the horror of his deed at the very instant at which his reality seems to elude him. He has killed without knowing that he was killing, and without the victim having uttered the slightest protest. He has killed with an ordinary action that, before this scene, had never resembled a murderous act. And so the only "proof" we have of the reality of the crime lies in the fact that the murderer felt slightly more muscular fatigue than usual in his forearms.[35] There exists in fact no other external trace of the deed: Hélène did not cry out at the moment of her passage from life to death; she seems not to have suffered; and her neck later showed no apparent marks of strangulation. The murder thus bore the traits of a perfect crime, except for the fact that instead of trying to hide it, the killer took the blame by telling his doctor he had done it, which the doctor found hard to believe.

But if such an act could take place, it was perhaps because certain events had occurred some time before, steering the two protagonists of the drama toward its catastrophe.[36]

Louis Althusser had undergone surgery to remove a hiatal hernia that was making it impossible to breathe when he ate. He tells of the profound mental derangement this produced in him. He was vomiting all the time, urinating in an irregular fashion, and losing his grip on language to the point of mixing up words; on top of that, he was persuaded that the Red Brigades had condemned him to death and were about to burst into his hospital room to finish him off. It was in this state that he returned to the ENS: "This whole 'pathological' system was compounded by suicidal delirium. Condemned to death and threatened with execution, I had only one resource: to forestall the infliction of death by killing myself in advance. I imagined all manner of mortal exits, and moreover I wanted not only to destroy myself physically but to wipe out all trace of my time on earth: in particular, to destroy every last one of my books and all my notes, and burn the École Normale, and also, 'if possible,' suppress Hélène herself while I still could."[37]

I recall that at this time Louis Althusser visited me often, sometimes with Hélène. He did in fact talk about setting the ENS on fire; he wanted to get away, and tried desperately to buy my apartment, to the point of persuading himself, and convincing Hélène, that I had put it up for sale. No rational argument had any effect in getting him to renounce this project. And yet, as soon as one broached another matter, something to do with politics or philosophy, this erratic behavior vanished.

It was at this period too—and I was a witness—that Althusser was beset with the conviction that humanity as a whole was going into decline and that some way had to be found to save it. Hélène held the same certainty. So it was that he renewed his attempts, but with greater urgency and after trying to alert public opinion by proposing schemes for meetings at the Mutualité, to gain an audience with Pope John Paul II and inform him that the crisis that was putting the salvation of the world at risk could only be resolved if a lasting dialogue between Rome and Moscow were initiated. Louis Althusser, like Jacques Lacan before him, had made many attempts to speak with the pope—clearly an attempt to unite, in a fusional act, the two tutelary figures of his history: Catholicism and communism. But this time, in the depths of his delirium, he had the presentiment that the battle being waged by the Polish pope was already won in the East. When Jean Guitton asked the Holy Father to receive the philosopher, he replied: "I know your friend; he is a logician above all, who pursues a line of thought to its conclusion. I will be happy to receive him."[38]

During the months that followed, Althusser and his wife shut themselves up in the closed chamber of an organized solitude. She called him a monster or complained of the intolerable suffering he had always caused her, according to which phase of her ritual alternation between bursts of mania and bouts of melancholy she happened to be in. "The limit was reached one day when she matter-of-factly asked me to kill her myself, and this word, unthinkable and intolerable in its horror, caused my whole body to tremble for a long time. It still makes me tremble. . . . We were living shut up in the cloister of our hell, both of us."[39]

But Althusser is not content, in his autobiography, just to portray the shattering reality of the great murder scene in its raw state. Putting to use his own experience of psychoanalytic treatment, he retraces in Freudian, and often Lacanian, terms the genealogical structure of a drama that he believed had forged, across three generations, the singular madness of a subject born to a family of the middling Catholic bourgeoisie exiled to Algeria after the defeat at Sedan in 1870.

At the beginning of the twentieth century a young girl, Lucienne Berger, was in love with a young man named Louis Althusser. A younger son, he was his mother's favorite and gave every promise of achieving intellectual success. His older brother, Charles, more boorish and less admired, was engaged to Juliette, Lucienne's sister. When the war came Louis was called up, and died in a reconnaissance airplane in the skies over Verdun. The two families then decided to obey the ancient biblical custom of the levirate, still current in the Mediterranean world at that time, which obliged an older, still unmarried, brother to wed the widow of a deceased younger brother. So Charles Althusser took Lucienne Berger for his wife, and when a child was born they gave him the name of his uncle Louis. The "madness" of this marriage lay less in its obedience to the tradition of the levirate than in its excessive obedience, outstripping the strict requirement. Nothing actually compelled Charles to wed Lucienne, because his younger brother had not yet married her. The younger Louis Althusser writes: "I had no father, and I endlessly played the game of 'father of the father' to give myself the illusion of having one, in fact to assign myself the role of a father with respect to my own self. . . . I had thus philosophically to become my own father as well. And that was only possible through conferring upon myself the fatherly function par excellence: domination and *mastery* of any possible situation."[40]

In thus instantiating the Sartrean idea of the absence of the superego (and the Sartrean rejection of the father), Althusser saw himself as having been given the name of a dead man: that of his uncle Louis. He extracted from this the thesis that all real theorists, especially the three "damned" thinkers of the late nineteenth century—Nietzsche, Freud, and Marx—had been forced to be fathers to their own selves. In identifying with them, he was emphasizing that only a tearing free from the symbolism of filiation could lead to the achievement of a foundational act. Hence the idea, destined to become so central to his philosophical position, that a subject is always decentered from his or her ego, because the structure that determines him or her is an absent causality. Must one not, in order to tear free of oneself and save one's soul, dissolve into a history without historicity? But does one not then risk, through decentering, dissolving all subjectivity in the annihilation of oneself and the other?

It was in 1946 that Louis Althusser met Hélène Rytmann, a Jewish woman of Russian origin, eight years older than himself, whom his friends considered "a little crazy." In childhood she had been the victim of sexual abuse by the family doctor, who had burdened her with the task of administering lethal doses of morphine at intervals to her parents, who were both afflicted with an incurable illness. "This frightful daughter had thus killed the father who loved her and whom she loved. . . . This frightful daughter had also killed the mother who detested her. At age thirteen!"[41] In the Resistance she had been a comrade of Jean Beaufret and the Pericles network and had subsequently joined the French Communist Party. She had been evicted from the party for reasons that remain unclear, though formally she was accused of "Trotskyist deviation" and "crimes." She had, it was said, taken part in the summary execution of former collaborators in the region of Lyon.[42]

In sharing the life of such a woman, Althusser was confronted every day with a destiny that, in certain respects, brought him ceaselessly back to himself while at the same time contradicting his own commitment. Hélène had been in the Resistance while he, as a prisoner of war, was remote from the anti-Nazi combat; she was Jewish and bore on her own person, in her history, all the stigmata of the Shoah, whereas he, despite his conversion to Marxism, never escaped the formative effect of integrist Catholicism. Finally, she became a victim of Stalinism at just the time when he was preparing to bind his conceptual thought to the history of the communist movement. In other words, Hélène was something like his own displaced conscience, pitiless superego, heterogeneous impulsion, damned part, black animality, impenetrable body perverted by a detestable mother. "She retained atrocious memories of her mother, who . . . never took her in her arms. Her mother hated her because she was expecting a boy, and this dark-complexioned daughter upset all her plans and wishes . . . : nothing but hate. . . . I had never embraced a woman, and above all I had never been embraced by a woman (at age thirty!). Desire mounted in me, we made love on the bed, it was new, exciting, exalting, and violent. When she (Hélène) had left, an abysm of anguish opened up in me, never again to close."[43]

But at the same time, and in a reverse movement, Hélène also represented for him not just the unattractive, dark-complexioned girl, author and abused victim of a double parricide but also the sublimated figure of his own hated mother to whom he remained attached all his life. "If I was dazzled by Hélène's love and the miraculous privilege of knowing her and having her in my life, I tried to give that back to her in my own way, intensely and, if I may put it this way, *as a religious offering*, as I had done for my mother."[44]

In consequence, the love that Hélène Rytmann inspired in Louis Althusser for thirty-five years was made of the same turmoil, the same putting to death, the same repulsion, the same exaltation, and the same fusion that united him at the same time with the Communist Party, the asylum, and psychoanalytic discourse. The destiny of the philosopher of Marxist melancholy can, in this regard, be compared to that of certain great mystics of Islam and Christianity, who in some cases wanted to found a singular liberty through the abolition of the Law and the creation of a community "without a subject," while others contested the principle of individual unity, the privilege of consciousness, and the myth of progress.[45]

Unlike Hélène, the other women loved by Louis Althusser were generally of great physical beauty and sometimes exceptionally sensitive to intellectual dialogue.[46] Thus, in the letters he wrote to Franca Madonia between 1961 and 1973, which were published prior to his autobiographical narrative, the reader finds the evocation of a passion that might have led to another murder scene, had it not been contained by any kind of sublimation. Thus, in an identical movement, and in the sumptuous decor of a dream Italy that might have been filmed by Bernardo Bertolucci, the wildness of infatuation and the limitless quest for a desire that only words could restrain were united for a time:

Franca, black one, night, fire, beautiful and ugly, extreme passion and reason, excessive and wise. . . . My love, I am broken by loving

you, my legs cut off this evening so that I can no longer walk—
and yet what else have I done today except think of you, pursue
you, love you? . . . An infinite march to exhaust the space you open
to me. . . . I say this, my love, I say this true thing—but I say it as
well to combat my desire for you, for your presence, the desire to
see you, speak to you, touch you. . . . If I write you, it is for that as
well, you have understood it so well: writing renders present in a
certain fashion, it is a struggle against absence.[47]

A philosopher, translator and playwright, Franca belonged to a well-
off Italian bourgeois family from Romagna. Her brother, a Marxist militant, went to work in the Alfa Romeo factory at Varese in 1967. As for
her husband, Mino Madonia, whose sister Giovanna was married to the
painter Leonardo Cremonini, he was a member of the Italian Communist Party, despite being the manager of a firm specializing in the production of felt hats.

Every summer the two families gathered at Villa Madonia, a charm-
ing residence situated in the village of Bertinoro, on the confines of the
Marche region and the province of Bologna, several kilometers from
Forlì. It was in this magical setting, surrounded by lemon trees, olean-
ders, and cedars of Lebanon, awash in ocher light and the strong odor
of vineyards, that Louis Althusser fell in love with Franca, discovering
through her everything he had missed in his own childhood and that he
lacked in Paris: a real family, an art of living, a new manner of thinking,
speaking, desiring.

In sum, at the heart of this relationship with this foreigner who translated the works of the great French authors (Lévi-Strauss, Merleau-
Ponty) and who made him appreciate modern theater (Pirandello,
Brecht, Beckett), he learned to detach himself from the Stalinist tradition
of communism, and thus to read the works of Marx *another way*. Out of
this strangeness activated by a woman—by *another woman*, or rather by
a womanhood that transcended his desire for confinement—out of this
cleavage induced by the alternation of geographical locations and finally
out of this interior exile lived in the mode of the dispossession of the
self, there welled up not only his finest texts (*For Marx* especially) but

also his most important concepts, like symptomatic reading, overdetermination, the trial without a subject.

The dazzlement lasted four years, from 1961 to 1965. Letters, telephone calls, trips, and meetings were the pretexts for philosophical and literary flights articulated in two languages, in which were mixed, in spoken and written words, opinions on current events, politics, and theory, and confidences on the happinesses and unhappinesses of daily life.

Very soon, though, Althusser started to want to inscribe this liaison in the web of psychical confinement that was causing him to oscillate between two models of femininity: the first, guilty and depressing, represented by his companion in Paris, the never-ending victim and object of compassion or repulsion; the second, initiatory and incandescent, incarnated by the foreigner who always projected a sort of Viscontian Italianness. So he tried to oblige Franca to become Hélène's friend, just as he sought to bring Mino into their exchanges. The result was an explosive situation, from which Franca succeeded in extricating herself.

If Louis Althusser was indeed the actor, throughout his life, in a scene of enclosure ever on the point of turning into a murder scene, he was also permanently the hero of a madness of infatuation that led him back every time inside a mystical circle from which sprang forth the most somber and exalted figures of his melancholy.

Confronted since 1948 with this saga of confinement, which he found echoed in Foucault's *History of Madness*, he maintained a relation to Freudianism as ambivalent as that with Marxism, maintaining a split between his status as psychiatrized analysand engaged in an orthodox cure and his position as theorist of psychoanalysis familiar with the Lacanian renewal.[48] On one hand he was the consenting and horrified victim of a chemical treatment against which he never ceased to rebel, on the other he saw himself as the defender of a doctrine of madness that denounced the principles to which he had voluntarily submitted. And likewise, every time he tried to escape the sealed chamber he had constructed with Hélène—by making the madness of infatuation alternate with the passion of sequestration—he did no more than reinvent the great journey of infinite lamentation that haunted him from childhood, from the time he had violently rejected his mother, his father, his ancestors, and along with them, later on, the very notion of family, the worst of the "ideological apparatuses of the state." In this respect the letters to Franca bear witness, as much as *The Future Lasts a Long Time* does, to Althusser's relation to psychoanalysis, to his own psychoanalytic cure, and to his main psychoanalyst, René Diatkine, himself a former analysand with Jacques Lacan.

The beginning of Althusser's analysis was preceded by an event that bore witness to the strange relationship between Hélène and her husband. In the summer of 1964, when she had just read the writings of Melanie Klein, she wrote Louis a letter in which she delivered herself of a striking interpretation of his "Oedipal" situation, reminding him especially of the extent to which his father had been an intruder and a "false husband" to his mother: "May one then say that the child is going to find himself compelled to be his own father?"

Fifteen days later Althusser noted the content of a murderous dream in his private notebooks:

I must kill my sister[49] or she must die. . . . Kill her with her own consent, as far as that goes: a sort of pathetic communion in sacrifice (. . . I would say, almost like an aftertaste of love-making, like uncovering the entrails of my mother or sister, her neck, her throat, to do her good). . . . Why is it my sister I must kill in the dream? no doubt fear of killing the other in the sexual act, fear of falling, through the sexual act, into the domain of death held by my mother, my sister, etc. as the domain of death. To accomplish the sexual act is to kill (the image of the other, the image of the mother). Crime in the effusion, in the warmth. . . . I will thus kill her with her consent and by her consent (and I will do it to the best of my ability), I am not guilty.[50]

Two months later, and nine months after having brought Lacan's seminar to the ENS, he began his analysis with Diatkine, with whose anti-Lacanian stance he was perfectly well acquainted. In January 1965 the sessions became more frequent, and in June the real work of exploring the unconscious was launched. He was soon telling Franca about the positive effects of this "orthodox" psychoanalysis. In July 1966 he affirmed that the treatment was yielding "spectacular results."

Now at that date Diatkine also took Hélène into therapy, while assuming the burden of the ongoing psychiatric care of his patient. A pathological relationship then came about between Althusser and his analyst, making the transference all the more constrictive and impossible to unbind in that Hélène's parallel analysis was helping to weld tighter the union, already dangerously fusional, between the philosopher and his companion, through which psychoanalytic knowledge served as a basis for wild interpretations. As a result Althusser felt galvanized into a state of all-powerfulness as "father of the father." He "played" the analyst: with Hélène by explaining her "case" to her (since she was explaining his to him), and with Franca by talking about Hélène's case with her. Simultaneously he posed as intellectual tutor to Diatkine, going so far as to ridicule him by giving him lessons in Lacanism: "Why do you give way to your impulse to repress the oeuvre of Lacan? It is an error, a fault that you ought not to commit, and yet that you do commit. You answer me by adducing Lacan's personality, but that is not the point: it is a question of his oeuvre. . . . It is a question of the existence of the right to theory in the analytic domain. Paris was certainly worth a mass. Between us, the 'personality' of Lacan, his 'style' and his manias, and all the effects they have produced, including personal wounds, are all worth it for his theory."[51]

Throughout this interminable psychoanalysis, Althusser succeeded with brio in occupying the position of "analyst of the analyst." The consequence of this was that he no longer separated his destiny from that of Hélène, while distancing himself from Franca and the Bertinoro circle. The two lovers continued to correspond, but as the years passed the tone changed: the love remained but desire fragmented, and the ideal of a new order of the world of which they had dreamed grew dim as the desire for a more vigorous commitment disintegrated. In 1970, in a letter with premonitory overtones, Franca wrote: "Do you know that Jack the Ripper not only strangled women, but tore out their viscera and hung them like garlands around the body and the bed?"[52]

The last letter addressed to Franca by Althusser, dated August 1973, reveals that the work of fusion with Hélène, heightened by analysis, had by now reached its limit: "If I stopped playing, I would stop myself in a manner as aggressive as my game itself. . . . H. for her part is going through a very bad analytic 'passage.' . . . The result was that our stay in Brittany, in which we were together twenty-four hours out of twenty-four, was marvellous as far as the countryside went, but catastrophic for our shared life."[53]

Althusser's autobiography could have been called *The Murder Scene*. This unclassifiable, undefinable text, unruly and unregulated, resembles no other, neither Rousseau's *Confessions* nor an ordinary pathography, nor even a clinical document interpretable by a rational consciousness in the same way, for example, as the *Memoirs of My Nervous Illness* by Daniel Paul Schreber, which Freud analyzed so well,[54] or as the clinical document drafted in the nineteenth century by Pierre Rivière, who murdered his mother, his sister, and his wife, commented upon by Michel Foucault and his team.

In truth, and although it was subtly constructed both as an homage to Sartre's *Words* and as a Dionysiac challenge to his own *For Marx*, *The Future Lasts a Long Time* cannot be qualified as literary narrative, psychiatric document, autofiction, or autobiography in any strict sense. Composed by an author whose consciousness vacillates while retaining an implacable lucidity, it presents the story of a delirious life of which the hero is both object and subject, divided between a *cogito* that places him outside his own madness and a madness that sends him back into the interiority of his *cogito*, split between a figure of compassionate femininity that drives him to murder and an imaginary of feminine passion that never succeeds in tearing him free of melancholy.

So there is nothing astonishing in the fact that this hero, the narrator of himself, can present himself, *from his death*, as the magistrate who is judging his crime, as the doctor who is conceptualizing his case, as the philosopher who is deconstructing communism, and as the madman who is accounting for the genealogy of his madness with the most scientific terminology of psychoanalysis and psychopathology.

A real challenge to reason, written at speed, and unadorned with the literary qualities one finds in many of Althusser's other works, this unnameable text, unique in the annals of philosophy, was logically bound to make anyone who ventured to comment upon it rave deliriously themselves.

It has to be said as well that no other piece of writing ever aroused such detestation. Aside from the literary critics who eagerly celebrated both the ruin of Marxism, which they made responsible for the Gulag, and the downfall of its last philosopher, necessarily an assassin too and so heaped with infamy, other adversaries, commentators, psychiatrists, philosophers, and psychoanalysts all piled on merrily.

In a style of great vulgarity, and brushing aside all respect for fact, the psychoanalyst Daniel Sibony adopted the widespread view that it was a case of premeditation, explaining that the philosopher had been compelled to "smother" his "other half" in order to signify how much the Marxist truth she incarnated, and of which she had been the "implacable Virgil" for him,

> deserved to be "eclipsed so that the other part of truth could finally be envisaged." . . . But the passage could not be accomplished without the gesture of madness in which however a whole stretch of History was driven and hallucinated; well before the thaw in Russia and the end of the USSR, this philosopher went ahead and carried it out with his own hands: by twisting the neck of the very soviet union in which he was confined with his wife; so as to protect himself from what might be coming. His eastern bloc could not be split without it starting to come unblocked and finally grasping the other aspect of his truth.[55]

From a quite different intellectual vantage point, Eugénie Lemoine-Luccioni set about massacring the autobiography of the philosopher (whom she apparently imagined to be alive in 1992, since she refers to him as having just published the work). Struck, evidently, by the fact that Althusser had dared, in a rigorously Lacanian fashion, to act as his own analyst, and ignorant of the relationship he had had with Lacan, she accused him of understanding nothing about the question of the symptom. While attacking Derrida's notion that "a letter doesn't always reach its destination," and without in the least understanding what Derrida meant, she retailed a baseless anecdote right out of an idolatrous imaginary: "An analysand of Lacan to whom Althusser confided his perplexity—for there are some letters that get lost, evidently—repeated what he had said to Lacan. Lacan reflected for a good while, it seems, then answered: 'Althusser is not a practitioner.' A luminous reply!"[56]

For their part, two psychiatrists, Michel Bénézech and Patrick Lacoste, employing a psychopathological discourse worthy of Père Ubu, published a close commentary on the philosopher's "uxoricide," positing that the strangulation had been caused not by the philosopher's state of depression but by a "conflict of love and hate between two persons: Althusser, to escape the anguish of separation and existential annihilation, must have preferred to kill the object of his attachment with his own hands, thus possessing it indefinitely in death."[57] And they professed their surprise that the philosopher had not been treated with lithium salts.

Knowing as one does that in fact Althusser swallowed enough lithium salts to make him choke, and observing that these two practitioners of psychosis and specialists in criminal psychiatry saw fit to mobilize a vocabulary right out of Melanie Klein in order to interpret the history of this tragedy in such a banal fashion, all the while remaining deaf to what a man had to tell about himself, one is driven to suppose that the book really was conceived by Althusser as a weapon of war for the purpose of turning, by its very rationality, the exponents of a discourse of assessment that is no more than a caricature of Freudian conceptuality into raving idiots themselves.

Another who resorted to the Kleinian approach was André Green, who roundly declared that Althusser had identified with a sadistic father to the point of taking himself for the protective and destructive mother of his students at the ENS. Green went on to correct the diagnosis of his psychiatrist colleagues, claiming that the philosopher was afflicted not with a "pure" manic-depressive psychosis, but with a more complex psychosis that supposedly led him to adopt a "psychotic lifestyle." He went on to stress that in Althusser there was by turns a murdered child and a dead child, and to posit that Hélène was a mother to him first, before becoming his father.

Finally Green gave an account of a meeting in the course of which he had used his psychiatric knowledge to bring supposed relief to the philosopher:

> Althusser's friends wanted a different analyst to take over from the one he was with. I was telephoned, the hope was expressed that I would help him to change analysts. . . . So I went to see him, out of affection and in order to say what I thought. Louis kept asking me repeatedly "But why did I kill Hélène, why, why?" I finally answered: "You killed Hélène so as not to kill your analyst." At that moment he received my interpretation as though he were thunderstruck. "Quoi!" Then, with a haggard air he got up, went to sit on the edge of the bed, opened the drawer of the bedside table, and took out an enormous bar of chocolate, which he devoured avidly.[58]

Pointing out quite correctly that it was Althusser's habit to stuff his mother with chocolates, Green concluded on that basis that the philosopher was himself no more than a "fed mother" and that he was obsessed by fantasies of perpetual abandonment. And he declared himself satisfied with his interpretation, all the while affirming, in the face of the evidence, that it had had a beneficial effect on Althusser.[59]

Louis Althusser devoured food with relish, and he sometimes ate in an ostentatious fashion. He was always claiming that he wanted to change analysts. On numerous occasions he asked me for analysts' addresses, even insisting that he wanted to begin analysis with my mother, Jenny Aubry. But he made all these requests in a way that betrayed avoidance of, or flight from, the very idea of change. When he said these things, Althusser behaved as though what he was saying was being caused by some sort of hallucination independent of any alterity. And the more he swamped his interlocutor with requests, the more he arranged things so that the replies would be inoperative, already inscribed, that is, in a discursive organization the sole purpose of which was to perpetuate the circle of a highly ritualized confinement. For this reason, I adopted the practice of answering him only with concrete actions, like furnishing him with addresses or arranging, with no ulterior therapeutic intention, for him to meet those he wished to meet.

There is, consequently, no warrant for the assertion that in killing Hélène he wanted to avoid killing his analyst, while taking the place of a cannibal mother. But there is warrant for thinking that in inventing such an interpretation André Green was actually responding, in delusional fashion, to an interrogation that was meant to provoke him into uttering nonsense. Althusser knew perfectly well how much his interlocutor disapproved of his analyst's methods. For that matter, every time anyone tried to get involved in the transference relationship he maintained with Diatkine, he made a game of pretending he wanted to escape from it. And the game was always tragic.

One of the most far-fetched interpretations of the murder scene came from Jean Allouch. Stressing that Althusser's "imposture" had been to not ask Lacan to be his analyst, he asserted that, unlike Diatkine, Lacan would have taken the risk of not hospitalizing him and even letting him commit suicide if it came to that, so as not to give in to his pressure. Allouch then goes on: "Only one woman was able to make him show his worth, a Jew with the characteristic nose, a bundle of suffering, a piece of rubbish, she made him show his worth, it is true, without being able to escape paying for it with her life. This added to Althusser's feeling of persecution . . . he called her *appareil idéologique de l'état* [ideological apparatus of the state] and abbreviated it 'AIE.' Of course the combination of these three letters was an acronym. But it is impossible not to transliterate it into the interjection 'aïe!' which Hélène Legotien-Rytmann never uttered."[60]

It is well known that Lacan was always inviting anyone and everyone to recline on his couch. Yet in his relations with Althusser he carefully avoided any such proposal. It is also well known that he never hesitated to commit a patient dangerous to himself or others to hospital. So there is warrant for thinking that Allouch's wordplay on "AIE/aïe," coupled with his reference of the most dubious kind to the discourse of anti-Semitism (the Jewish woman's nose), amounts to a very odd way of proceeding. It has less to do with the real murder scene than it does with the twisted reality of an author, Allouch, who makes a travesty out of the scene he claims to be commenting upon.

Once more then, Althusser's text serves to remind the official exponents of psychopathology that the rigor of psychoanalytic knowledge can sometimes allow a subject—be he the most demented of murderers—to reappropriate the meaning of his own destiny, at the cost of punishing himself with ten years of inner exile for the crime he committed and for which he assumed responsibility.[61]

But there is another reason this autobiography holds such a special place in the history of French philosophic discourse at the end of the twentieth century, provoking outbursts of rancorous hatred and idiotic nonsense: It subverts all the rules proper to this genre of narrative. Instead of playing the game of transparency, introspection, the quest for the self, and the revival of buried memories, Althusser presents himself before the reader in multiple facets, and leaps from one subject, and one epoch, to another. Sometimes he contradicts himself or commits errors of fact, even going so far as to say that he was an impostor, and that he had never read a line of Freud's oeuvre—even that he was scarcely acquainted with that of Marx. Adopting a carnivalesque pose,[62] he attempted to travesty his own thought, pretending in retrospect that it had all been a hoax.

Mixing intimate confession, fantasy, and the reflexive gaze, he never ceases to plant doubt in the minds of his future commentators, as though, knowing that he would never have to answer for what he was setting down—since he would be dead at the time of publication—he were wreaking vengeance, in a tone half tragic and half macabre, for having been put in the position of having to expound his own "case." Taking himself in structural fashion for the "father of the father," it was incumbent on him as well—and this is one of the main themes of the autobiography—to transmit a teaching, and so to draw up a balance sheet, addressed especially to his students and disciples, of what he had contributed to twentieth-century philosophy. It was incumbent on him to explain himself for posterity. The tempest had swept him up in the worst way possible, since, although he was a militant communist, he had never physically taken part in any combat: neither the anticolonialist struggle, nor that against Stalinism, of which he had nonetheless been the great deconstructor and fierce enemy. All his commitments came down to battles of the written word, punctuated by retreats into melancholy, and it was his coruscating writings that had gained him worldwide recognition, never any strictly political acts.

Consequently the act of 17 November 1980, or rather the surrender to the impulse to act that had turned him into a murderer, had become his major act, the only one indeed for which he had to answer. So the narrative of this act would necessarily supply the most authentic testimony on the meaning of a life and the import of an oeuvre.

To put it another way, it is because Althusser was willing to confront, in writing, the murder scene—or rather the reality of this unnameable scene—that he could render an accounting, *after the fact*, of his intellectual destiny. This, no doubt, is why the finest pages of the autobiography are those that recount his commitment to Marxism—a corporeal, physical, sexual, vital, fusional commitment. In the Spinozist theory of the body, in Machiavelli's *fortuna*, in the idea of an authority able to put an end to the "war of all against all" (from Hobbes to Rousseau), in the materialism of Marx, and in the purest forms of the concept of political action, he encountered, on each reading, and throughout the course of the collective work upon which he had embarked with his closest collaborators—friends or students—his own "experience of a body at first torn apart and lost, an absent body, everything of excessive fear and hope that there was in me, recomposed and, as it were, discovered. . . . That one might in this way regain the disposition of one's own body, and draw from this appropriation the wherewithal to think freely and strongly, thus properly speaking to think with one's body, in one's body even, of one's body, in sum that *the body might think* through and in the deployment of its strength, was truly amazing to me."[63]

This passionate plunge into conceptuality was accompanied by a certain ignorance of political reality in Althusser, so great was the gap between the space of interpretation and that of praxis. And so his body, so present in the elaboration of thought, fainted away whenever the risk arose of a confrontation with real events. While May 1968 was happening, Althusser, who had dreamed of the revolution, passed the spring and part of the summer confined in a clinic. Convinced that the French Communist Party had betrayed the working class by refusing to join the insurrection, he failed to see that the people had different demands from those of the student youth.

Seeking new subjective freedoms, the young contested the whole academic system: the professorial mandarins, the modes of transmitting knowledge, the rigidities of the old patriarchal authoritarianism, the barriers to the free unfolding of a sexuality without limits. Even if the rebels took over the words, concepts, and slogans of Marxist practice in aid of their struggle, they were already situating themselves outside that discourse. They spoke of their dreams using outdated and utterly dogmatic language, without perceiving the phase shift between a rhetoric that belonged to the past and aspirations already fixed on the near future.

Hence they reproached Althusser for remaining attached, body and soul, to a party headed for extinction, to a certain image of an outmoded communism of which they were themselves, much more than him, but only in appearance, the most archaic representatives. The upshot of this was that Louis Althusser did not succeed in transmitting any philosophical heritage. Oscillating between the internal criticism that condemned him to confinement and a subversive teaching that drove his students to act against him, he was the victim of his own blockages.

This explains why he suffered so keenly when the leadership of the French Communist Party decided to jettison the notion of the dictatorship of the proletariat, erasing it from their statutes.[64] You don't abandon a concept, he would say, the way you abandon a dead dog. He regarded this gesture as a theoretical disaster because to him it meant that a handful of bureaucrats had arrogated to themselves the right, arbitrarily and for opportunistic reasons, to inflict injury on a system of thought that was in a sense an integral part of his own body. To him it was like a killing and it plunged him once again into the tempest.

Three years after Althusser's death, Jacques Derrida was invited to give a lecture at the University of California on the topic "where is Marxism headed? Is it moribund?" The philosopher of deconstruction had never been either a Marxist or a communist or a member of any party. His commitments lay elsewhere. But the idea of discussing this subject, at a time when the Soviet system had entirely collapsed, gave him the chance to think about a new approach to the oeuvre of Marx.

It was not upon China, nor the eastern bloc countries, nor upon any communist, neocommunist, or postcommunist party that Derrida chose to focus his critical gaze. He preferred to reflect, in a manner both lyrical and Shakespearean, on the foundational work of Marx in relation to the history of communism. "A specter is haunting Europe: the specter of communism," Marx had written in the opening of the famous *Manifesto*. So what then is the nature, Derrida responded, of the new specter haunting the maniacal and jubilant discourse of those who are today proclaiming everywhere that Marx is dead, that his decomposing cadaver is safely stowed away, and that never again will he turn up to disturb the good conscience of the West?

Specters of Marx is certainly one of Derrida's finest books, and one understands why it was a worldwide success. Rather than being turned toward the past, or nostalgically evoking a bygone era, it sounds a call to a new struggle against the triumphant powers of the technosciences, which are using the pretext of the death knell of the Marxist period to impose a globalized order in which man will be no more than a piece of merchandise meant for enslavement all the more bitter for being decked out as the fulfillment of the democratic ideal:

> For one must cry out, at a time when some dare to neo-evangelize in the name of a liberal democracy finally fully realized as the ideal of human history: instead of hymning the advent of the ideal of liberal democracy and the capitalist market in the euphoria of the end of history, instead of celebrating the "end of ideologies" and the end of the great emancipatory discourses, let us never overlook this macroscopic obvious fact, composed of countless individual sufferings: no amount of progress warrants us to ignore the fact that never, in absolute terms, never have so many men, women, and children been enslaved, famished or exterminated on earth.[65]

As he was writing the lecture that was to become *Specters of Marx*, Derrida was thinking of South Africa, which had just renounced apartheid. He knew that a communist militant had just been assassinated there: "I remind you that it was a *communist as such*, a *communist as communist*, that a Polish immigrant and his accomplices, all the assassins of Chris Hani, put to death a few days ago. The killers themselves declared that they went after a communist. So they tried to interrupt negotiations and sabotage a negotiation that was under way. . . . Let me salute the memory of Chris Hani and dedicate this lecture to him."[66]

In this profoundly Freudian text, which opens with a call to hope—"I wish to learn to live at last"—Derrida renders a last homage, without explicitly saying so, to his friend Louis Althusser, to one who, after having led a spectral existence for ten years, had ended by being no more than the murderer of himself. Not a militant assassinated *for being a communist*, but a thinker of communism condemned to wander in the infernal circle of a universe of crime: crimes perpetrated in the name of communism, the killing of conceptuality, the murder of a woman of the Resistance, a militant of the communist idea.

5. GILLES DELEUZE

{ANTI-OEDIPAL VARIATIONS}

"ONE DAY, PERHAPS, THE CENTURY WILL BE DELEUZEAN." Michel Foucault made this prophecy in 1969, when *Difference and Repetition* and *The Logic of Sense* were published.[1] The philosopher of the pathways of night was implying that, of all those with whom he had debated, Gilles Deleuze alone would one day have the privilege, not of entering the Pantheon or founding a school, but of being seen as one who had renewed philosophy, and thus as one of the greatest of the moderns.

Strongly committed to the left, never having been either a phenomenologist or a critical reader of Heidegger, Deleuze was also the only one of the six whose destinies I am evoking never to have been a student at the École Normale Supérieure. He was simply a professor of philosophy,[2] in the lycées of Amiens and Orléans, then in Paris at the Lycée Louis-le-Grand and at the Sorbonne, then in Lyon, and finally, after May 1968, at the University of Paris VIII, at that time located in Vincennes, where he "invented" day by day, before his astonished students and in contact with Félix Guattari, his most iconoclastic book: *Anti-Oedipus*.[3]

Intent on commenting on the texts of the great philosophers, he posed at first as a historian of philosophy of sorts who criticized the idea that the teaching of the history of philosophy might pose an obstacle to the creation of concepts. But he also saw himself as belonging to a generation that had literally been assassinated with the history of philosophy: "You won't, all the same, dare speak in your own name as long as you haven't read this or that, and that on this, and this on that."[4]

For many years his manner of conceiving and teaching the history of philosophy was to regard it as a sort of "sodomy [*enculage*], or, what amounts to the same thing, immaculate conception." He imagined himself "mounting an author from behind and getting him pregnant with a child that would be his, but monstrous."[5] And then, his reading of the oeuvre of Nietzsche, as well as his exceptional relationship with literary texts, films, popular song, and painting, caused him to evolve toward a questioning, not destructive but critical or even deconstructive, of all the major constituted knowledges. Derrida said: "Deleuze certainly remains, despite many divergences, the one among all those of this 'generation' to whom I have always thought myself closest."[6]

Like Derrida and Foucault, Deleuze was detested. Accused like Socrates of wishing to corrupt youth with his teaching, he was also blamed for an immoderate love of drugs and alcohol. For having written *Anti-Oedipus* he was even compared to some kind of degenerate who had proffered "the defence of the rotten on the dungheap of decadence."[7] Finally, he was branded an anti-Semite for having protested against the banning of a film judged anti-Semitic by the Ministry of Culture and withdrawn from circulation. In protest at this censorship, Deleuze had indeed criticized all the associations that had arrogated to themselves the right to judge the content of a work of art, however problematic, without having debated it, without even being capable of debating it.[8]

The fact is, he disconcerted his interlocutors and readers with a paradoxical attitude that always seemed to run counter to rational discourse. Deleuze was the philosopher of extremes and of laughter, of the grotesque and the sublime, of dream and desire. Without being the slightest bit romantic, he was animated by a sort of incandescent passion for creative genius that made him receptive to the most utopian, but also the subtlest, manifestations of art, poetry, and literature.

He had no hesitation, for example, in advocating a mechanistic materialism centered on the idea that there exists a strong linkage between psychical activity and brain activity. Unlike Canguilhem, who had been his master and whom he admired, he thought that science would one day make it possible to demonstrate, through cerebral imaging, that the brain is capable—in itself and apart from any subjectivity—of creating concepts and works of art. But despite that, he never endorsed the simplistic approaches of the adepts of scientism, cognitivism, and cerebral psychology, and for that matter took the view that any comparison between human behavior and animal behavior was a step in the direction of fascism. And to subvert the very idea of such an approach, he readily declared that this type of human relation to the animal horrified him, and that the only important thing in his eyes was the becoming animal of man, that man should prove his capacity to think the animal in terms of animality so as to expose himself to that which exceeds him.[9]

Deleuze, like his friend Foucault, despised medical power, detested any form of religion of science, and, like Canguilhem, considered normative psychology a barbarous discipline. He could not bear the idea, dominant today, that a human being can be "assessed," instrumentalized, reduced to a thing, to the least of humans, and, worse than that, to the least of things: inert matter, detritus. He, a sufferer from tuberculosis living on borrowed time, believed that every individual subject ought to be able to consume his drugs and medicines freely with the aid of his physician—and not under the domination of an alienating power. Every individual, he said, has the right to choose his destiny, even if it puts his life at risk. A subject is only a subject because he is first of all a nonsubject, that is to say a multiple and ever-deterritorialized singularity.

Deleuze was, finally, the most "antisecurity" philosopher one can imagine, the most anticonformist, the most corrosive, the most refractory to all the attempts at destruction (of culture, of nature, of man) that have become the common lot of our age—an age whose onset he had foreseen. Hence he had the greatest admiration for the subversive power of Sartre's discourse: "Sartre is a redoubtable polemicist. . . . There is no genius without self-parody. But what is the best parody? To become a conformist elder, a clever, coquettish authority? Or to aim to be the hold-out of Liberation? To fancy oneself an academician, or dream of being a Venezuelan guerrilla fighter?"[10]

But since he was not an adept of limitless gratification (always ruinous, he used to say) Deleuze liked to emphasize that philosophy should never let itself be used by one doctrine for the purpose of destroying another: no struggle to the death, but the necessity for conflict and the search for that which may be the most conflictual in oneself and in others.

From the same perspective, he asserted that the ingestion of harmful substances ought to be interrupted if the subject was turning into a wreck incapable of working. That was the limit. At that point, he turned into the good moralist, advocating abstinence and self-control. In the same spirit, Deleuze reproached the representatives of medical power, especially psychiatrists, with fabricating, in their hospitals, through senseless and excessive prescribing and the exercise of a psychopathological diktat, veritable mental patients depossessed of their "true" madness.

Consequently he rejected, not medical science as such, not the biological approach to the psyche, but every form of medicalization of existence At all events, Deleuze never propagandized for the use of dangerous substances and never encouraged his students to use drugs. I can bear witness to this because I was his student and did not share his views. He didn't judge, he didn't normalize. What interested him in love, in friendship, and in the teaching he did, was to grasp the portion of shadow and heterogeneity proper to each individuality, its portion of hubris. He thought that only the exercise of depersonalization, in other words the opening up to multiplicities, allows every person to speak in his own name.

Deleuze thereby located himself within a tradition, both Spinozist and perfectly ethical, that respects to the highest degree the suffering of all "minorities," the mad, the vagrants, the marginal, the homosexuals. In certain respects this great philosopher of the untimely, of fibrils, and of the decentering of symbolic orders continued Victor Hugo's fine tradition of compassion not only for the poor and the disinherited but also for those who had always been the victims of social, political, racial, and sexual persecution: the "insulted" victims, the ones treated like garbage.

Didier Eribon, a knowledgeable Deleuzean, supplies a moving piece of testimony to the sort of abject abuse that Deleuze so hated. Unlike the kind instituted or authorized by repressive powers, this kind of abuse conceals itself under a cloak of utter normality in democratic societies: ordinary acts, impossible to combat. Eribon writes:

> We stand on the sidewalk for a few moments outside the door [of a gay bar], debating whether to go in. A car comes along with the windows rolled down: four or five youths inside bellow insults at us: "*Pédés, pédés* . . . [fags, fags]." The car stops and one of the occupants spits on me before I can draw back. The dribbles of spit form a kind of silver star on my blue polo shirt. My body reacts with a retch (physical) of disgust. I am on the point of vomiting. . . . I recall what Georges Dumézil told me about the day when, during the war, he went to visit his master and friend Marcel Mauss and saw for the first time the yellow star sewn onto his clothing. He could not take his eyes off this frightful stigma. The great sociologist then remarked to him: "You are looking at my gob of spit." For a long time I understood this phrase in the most straightforward way: Mauss meant that he considered this bit of yellow cloth as a dirty stain, a piece of filth thrown in his face. But eventually someone pointed out to me that I was mistaken: Mauss had doubtless used the word "*crachat*" [literally, "gob of spit"] in the sense of "decoration." And indeed, one of the old demotic meanings of the word "*crachat*" is that of insigne, medal, or decoration.[11]

Inhabited by an inner wound of which he never spoke, out of hostility toward any reduction of life to a "little private affair," Deleuze foresaw the arrival of a one-dimensional world without culture and without soul, entirely subject to the laws of the market and the politics of things,[12] a sort of factory for making wretches, modern avatars of Cosette, Jean Valjean, Thénardier, and Javert.

Even before conceptualizing this expression he had grasped its signifying power when, in the summer of 1936, at age eleven, he had observed in his own family the great fear felt by the bourgeoisie at the unexpected upsurge of those thousands of men and women, factory workers, who were for the first time invading "their" territory: beaches, seasides, rivers, highways, fields, multiple and multiplied spaces, endless countryside in which to take long bicycle rides.

This transgressive spectacle left him with the memory of a France divided in two: the one reactionary, patriarchal, familist, and territorialized that he always abhorred and that he knew would never pardon the "Jew" Léon Blum for having thus infringed on its geographic privileges; the other rhizomatic, machinelike, deterritorialized, and with which he very soon felt the urge to identify as he watched the films of Jean Renoir with delight or listened to the songs of Charles Trenet and Édith Piaf. He later became an attentive reader of Proust, Sacher-Masoch, Lewis Carroll, and many others.

The factory versus the theater, the free-running pack versus the closed field of the ego-logical and superego-ic zoo, the continents versus the nations, the subversion of fluxes against barbed wire and borders, the frivolity of the ever-rippling fold versus the fixity of the smooth, perfectly ironed fabric: such were the fruits of the formidable inventiveness of the Deleuzean factory. The philosopher of the rhizome exploded the classic representations proper to philosophic discourse, preferring to move down the hidden ways of a primitive scene, a veritable machine for making concepts, rather than endlessly reinventing the genealogy of Hamlet, Antigone, or Oedipus in commentaries.

Deleuze liked neither the tragic, nor its dramaturgy, nor the schools of thought—be they Socratic, Aristotelian, Wittgensteinian, or Freudian—because they continually threatened, he used to say, to kill off creativity by reducing singularities to families, to organized collectivities. Neither did he think that desire could be "liberated" by spontaneous action. He maintained rather, and in a sophisticated way, that desire itself is a work of the unconscious, of an unconscious conceived as an ordering of animal and musical territories,[13] not like a theater or some "other stage."

He had likewise retained, from his reading of the oeuvre of Nietzsche, the idea that it was necessary to overturn Platonism in order to find, behind the simulacra of ideas and repetitions of ideas, a Dionysian chaos composed of pain, joy, and disorder, festive and untimely chaos: "It is not in great forests or on footpaths that philosophy is elaborated, but in cities and streets, including in that which is most *factitious* in them."[14] With this gesture he attempted to link an ontology of multiplicity to a politics of the event,[15] and it was to Heraclitus that he referred to show that nothing is ever repeated identically—one never steps in the same river twice—and that all phenomena are always multiple, fluxes irreducible to unicity.[16]

For all those who, like me, knew Félix Guattari and took part in the dazzling seminar that Deleuze held at Vincennes between 1969 and 1972, *Anti-Oedipus* is a great book. It testifies as well to the fact that in expressing their joint will to overturn dogmas through a sole authorial voice, the two friends gave the psychoanalytic conformism of the time a lesson in pleasure, revolt, and liberty that one would wish to see revived today—in different forms, naturally.

By this time Deleuze already had his famous "desiring machines" in his head. As for Guattari, his project was different from Foucault's: Like the English and Italian antipsychiatrists, but on a different conceptual basis, he wanted to pose, and perhaps resolve, the problem of the nature of madness. Is it a mental illness or a singular revolt that aims to overturn the established order?

So the two friends set about constructing the *Anti-Oedipus*, as if composing an opera, through an exchange of letters in which they addressed each other with courteous formality as *vous* instead of the familiar *tu*. With its long-range writing dominated by rhizomatic rhetoric, the work, even on the formal level, set against the imperialism of the *One*—that is, of the symbolic structure or order—a machinelike and plural essence of desire, a factory of impulses and phantasms uniquely capable of subverting the ideals of an Oedipal and patriarchal sovereignism.

Between Gilles and Félix, the one a sedentary and Nietzschean Socrates with an admirable mastery of language and thought, the other always on the move and scattered, simultaneously inhabiting several spaces, themselves multiple, the marriage was beneficial, since it gave birth to this book that continues to be read, translated, and commented upon throughout the world, even if its composition remains, *despite all*, enigmatic. (Today, though, we know that Deleuze took care of the final draft, though he always declared that without Guattari he would never have written it, any more than he would their other collaborative works.) "Be the pink panther," said the two authors, "and may your loves be like the wasp and the orchid, the cat and the baboon."[17]

Every week at the University of Vincennes Deleuze told his students about the adventures of a book that seemed to be writing itself all alone on the stream of a feverish and open word. *Anti-Oedipus* was there in the middle of the classroom like a multiple god expanding in the heart of each one of the protagonists fascinated by the Deleuzian chant, by the tonality of a voice unlike any other.

The philosopher of packs and of the multiple asserted that he wished to rethink the history of human societies, starting with the postulate that capitalism, tyranny, and despotism would run up against their limits in the desiring machines of a "successful" schizophrenia, one entirely free of the grip of psychiatric discourse: a madness in the free state, disalienated. Around this point unfolded their great critique of psychoanalysis, their offensive against the most psychologized monument of the Freudian edifice, the Oedipus complex. As manipulated by Freud's descendants, they said, it was no longer a revisitation of the ancient tragedy but a machine for normalizing the libido and erecting a retrograde familist ideal.[18]

To escape from this psychologization of existence, the authors proposed to substitute a polyvalent conceptuality capable of conveying the machinelike essence of a plural desire for all the structural, symbolic, and signifying theories issuing from psychoanalysis. Against the imperialism of the unique signifier, and against the totalizing Oedipus, Deleuze proposed a schizoanalysis grounded in a psychiatry described as materialist and Marxist in inspiration. "A materialist psychiatry is one that introduces production into desire, and inversely desire into production. Delirium bears not on the father, or even on the name of the father, it bears on the name of History. It is like the immanence of desiring machines in the great social machines."[19]

Since it aspired to a great synthesis of the ideals of liberation, the work logically took the psychoanalytic conformism of the time (especially Lacanian dogmatism) as its main target, along with all the catechisms of Oedipal psychology. But since Guattari belonged to the Lacanian community, and to a psychiatric tradition issuing from institutional and dynamic psychotherapy, it did not produce any revolution in the clinical approach to the psychoses.

On the other hand it was received as an innovative work by all those who thought that life itself was nothing more than a passage through a chaotic experience. Deleuze joyfully went after all the ideologies of the end of history and the end of man, denouncing their nihilism and their reactionary character. The human animal, he said in substance, must confront that which exceeds him—his most extreme passions and desires—that is to say, the Multiple and the clamor of being, on pain of sinking into a new form of servitude: the invisible neofascism of the One, always at work in the most apparently democratic societies.[20]

The anti-Oedipal program was of course never realized. Rather than contest the familial order, all those who were excluded from it—the homosexuals especially—sought instead to become part of it so as to transform it from inside and invent a new politics of desire. As to the mad-people whom Deleuze and Guattari had wanted to liberate from the grip of Oedipal discourse, they never became heroes of social subversion. Treated with medications and subjected to the simplistic classifications of the new psychiatric order, they are today cataloged from the start as mentally ill and rarely regarded as Rimbauldian voyagers in search of multiple continents.

Too young to have taken part in the anti-Nazi struggle, Deleuze had been formed by classic philosophy and had admired Sartre, the emblematic figure of the anticolonial struggle, before joining Foucault's great battles in favor of minorities and the excluded. And it was through contact with Deleuze that the philosopher of the pathways of night had come to understand to what extent anti-Oedipalism might go beyond its critique of psychoanalysis and become the longed-for instrument of a deconstruction of the tendentially fascistic forms of human existence, individual and collective.

In this regard he was no doubt right to affirm that the century would one day, perhaps, be Deleuzean, because the century might one day, perhaps, come to resemble the nightmare imagined by Deleuze: the installation of an ordinary fascism, not the historic fascism of Mussolini and Hitler (so skilled in mobilizing the desire of the masses), but first and foremost "the fascism that is in all of us, that haunts our minds and our daily conduct, the fascism that makes us love power, desiring the very thing that dominates and exploits us."[21]

6. JACQUES DERRIDA

{THE MOMENT OF DEATH}

T HE TIME HAS COME TO BID FAREWELL (*ADIEU*) TO THE dead, to these philosophers of rebellion so different from one another, who never stopped arguing with and loving one another, and whose heirs, like it or not, we are. That is why I close this book by rendering homage to Jacques Derrida, to the man who was my friend for twenty years. The last survivor of this generation, he was the last to die, but also the only one to have bid his own farewell, in a book,[1] to most of those who formed this generation, and to many others as well, to which I add here a sort of postscript and so render my own homage in turn to what is immortal in friendship, to what is strongest in the fact of evoking the past the better to face the future: learning to think for tomorrow, learning to live, understanding what tomorrow will be made of.[2]

The law that governs the relationship that each subject maintains with the dead friend, and thus with death and friendship, is a structural and universal law, an "inflexible and fatal law: of two friends, one will see the other die."[3] This death, when it comes, is not just the end of such and such a life, but the "end of something in totality." In consequence, no mourning is possible. But since the absence of mourning always risks driving mad the friend who remains behind, only the state of melancholy permits the integration into oneself of the death of the other and the continuation of life.

I have had to confront such loss and I have had to compose farewells to dear ones and friends who have departed. And I have always said goodbye to the dead person right after his or her death. Never have I been able to write a funeral eulogy before the real death of those who were to die, even when they were condemned in advance by an implacable illness.

No one can ever, it seems to me, speak death before the coming of death. And when that does occur, when a farewell is written in advance, like a murder of death, the imposture is readable between the lines. The dead person is then deprived of the possible narrative of his death, and that death identified with a nothingness. Betrayal of chronology, betrayal of the time necessary for the approach of death, for its narration, for its celebration. Supreme transgression, finally, because this act of putting to death of death, perpetrated before death, makes the one who is composing the text the master—necessarily illusory—of a suspension of time. For nothing actually guarantees that the author of a necrology before death will not already be dead at the moment of the death of the one whose death he has related.

Ultimate separation, the farewell is spoken *from out of* life, as the moment at which are intermingled the death lived, the death undergone, the death celebrated, the memory of death. To say *adieu*, the make one's *adieux*, to make a visit of *adieu*, all these expressions really signify that he who is departing remits to God [*à Dieu*] the soul of the one who remains behind: *for ever*. To say farewell is also to disappear oneself, to cut oneself off from the world in which one had lived and accede to another world. But, to pronounce an *adieu*, to say *adieu* to a dead friend, may on the contrary also be, for the survivor, to remit *à Dieu* the soul of the departed one so that the memory of friendship may live beyond death, eternally. But this may also be to transform the *à Dieu* into an *adieu*, to pass discreetly from the kingdom of God to that of the death of God. The *à Dieu* presupposes the existence of God and the *adieu* his effacement. And it is no accident that the distinction between *adieu* and *au revoir* [until next we meet] came about in French usage at the beginning of the nineteenth century, in the aftermath of a revolution that had destroyed, with a regicide unique in the world, the bond that joined God to royal sovereignty. The *à Dieu* faded away, replaced by *adieu* and giving rise to *au revoir*. A century earlier people still said: *adieu, jusqu'au revoir*.

The execution of Louis XVI was not just the decapitation of a king but the putting to death of the monarchy. From out of life, and so that the nation might live, it was necessary, with no ceremony of farewell, with no remitting of the soul of the deceased *à Dieu*, with no *adieu, jusqu'au revoir*, to say *adieu* to royalty, which had become the kingdom of the dead.

As for mourning for the departed loved one, it never really takes place, and it was to give meaning to this impossibility that Freud felt the need, in 1915, to tie and untie, in the same movement, the bonds that unite mourning and melancholy. At the risk, in fact, of making melancholy not a subjective destiny but a pathology proper to narcissistic neuroses. Only with the discovery of the death wish, and the lived experience of the death of certain members of his family, especially his daughter and his grandson, was the master of Vienna able to accept the idea that certain mournings are impossible to perform. About the death of Sophie, he wrote: "One knows that after such a loss, the sharp grief will wane, but one always remains inconsolable, without finding a substitute. Everything that takes this place, even occupying it entirely, always remains other. And at bottom, it is better so. It is the only way to perpetuate this love, which one does not wish to abandon at any cost."[4] And: "It is true, I have lost my dear daughter, aged twenty-seven, but I have supported the loss strangely well. It was in 1920, one was worn down by the misery of war, prepared for years to find out that one had lost a son. Submission to destiny was thus prepared. . . . Since the death of Heinerle, I no longer love my grandchildren, and I no longer rejoice in life. This is also the secret of indifference. People have labelled this courage in the face of the threat to my own life."[5]

What these two passages, which nevertheless contradict one another, show is that the death of a rising generation, when not caused by war, epidemic, natural disaster, or massacre, is felt as a pathology. The rule of evolution does in fact dictate that the genealogical order should never be disturbed.[6] For it is written in the great book of time that a man should always disappear after his forebears and before his offspring. So the more death strikes against this apparently immutable destiny, the greater the suffering that invades the soul of the survivor forced to accept the unacceptable. From the end of the eighteenth century, and even more so at the end of the twentieth, the transgression of this rule has been experienced as an even more intense anomaly.[7]

Derrida's farewells are words torn from silence and nothingness: "*In memoriam*, the taste of tears, by dint of mourning, I shall have to wander all alone, friendship-before-all-else." And finally, about Lévinas: "But I have stated that I did not wish only to recall that which he entrusted to us of the *à Dieu*, but above all to say *adieu* to him, call him by his name, as he is called at the moment when, if he no longer responds, it is also that he responds in us . . . by reminding us: '*à-Dieu*' *Adieu* Emmanuel."[8]

Before a friend's tomb, before the dead one henceforth deprived of words, it is indeed a question of holding off the onset of mourning with a challenge. Of saying *adieu* and not *à Dieu*. And if "each time is unique," that means that everyone has the right to a singular salutation, which can also be the repetition of a same evocation of loss: "Too much to state, my heart fails, my strength fails, I must wander by myself, absence remains ever unthinkable to me henceforth, what is happening stops me breathing, how not to tremble? how to act? how to be? to speak is impossible, to remain silent also, what I thought was impossible is there before me, indecent, unjustifiable, intolerable, like a catastrophe that has already taken place and that must necessarily be repeated. I ask you to pardon me if today I have strength for no more than a few very simple words. Later I shall try to speak better." One could multiply ad infinitum the list of these mournful words that punctuate the farewells of Jacques Derrida to his friends, *des adieux sans Dieu*.

Without posing the question of the ways of dying in the West, without distinguishing between the various ways of dying—suicide, accident, illness, violent death, gentle death, longed-for death, sudden death, surrender to impulse—and whatever the age of the person to whom he ·

was addressing his salute, Jacques Derrida constructs his discourse like the palimpsest of the moment of death, like the instantaneous trace of that unique moment at which the passage from life to death comes about. Thus he is able to summon to himself the entire buried memory of a fragmented existence. Every time a detail surges up out of the darkness, so that the melody of the "inflexible and fatal" law may be enlivened: "To have a friend, to behold him, to follow him with your eyes, to admire him in friendship, is to know, in a manner a little more intense and wounded in advance, always insistent, more and more unforgettable, that one of the two will inevitably see the other die. One of us—each says—one of us two, one of these days, will see himself no longer seeing the other."[9]

The farewells of Jacques Derrida are thus neither funeral eulogies in the classic sense, nor necrologies, nor narratives of agony. It is not he who has chosen to speak the moment of death, or the degradation of the flesh, or the horror of the visage as it freezes or the corpse as it stiffens. He did not recount the last days of Emmanuel Kant, nor write a *Last Moments of Baudelaire* or a *Dying Voltaire*. He did not have to bear witness to any "ceremony of farewell."[10]

Nor did he gather together the words for death—perish, disappear, succumb, pass over, decease (the most horrible). And he did not portray graphically either the last moments of the ones condemned to die, nor the last words invented for death by the living awaiting death: "O death, old captain, it is time. Let us lift anchor." Or: "This idea of death installed itself definitively in me, as a love does." Or again: "Death, the masked specter, has nothing beneath his visor."[11] Neither infamous deaths nor illustrious deaths. Quite simply, death.

Derrida's farewells to his friends do not present either mortuary masks or the grand ceremonial of preparation for death. Between rupture and return, between the separation of "with God" and reintegration of the other into oneself, in sum, between the *adieu* and the *au revoir*, they allow us to understand, in an undertone, the pain and the fainting, and above all the narrative and almost ontological, structure of every recital of death and friendship: one person will have to disappear before the other. Thus they do not refer to the biographical trajectory of the loved being except through a writing of the parenthesis comparable to the cinematographic technique of the flashback.[12] Ever gasping, the word shatters in a perpetual unfulfillment: "Deleuze certainly remains, despite many divergences, the one among all those of this 'generation' to whom I have always thought myself closest. . . . And then I recall the memorable ten-day Nietzsche conference at Cerisy in 1972, and then so many other moments that make me, along with Jean-François Lyotard no doubt (who was there too), feel myself quite alone today, surviving and melancholy, out of what they call with a terrible and slightly false word, a 'generation.'"[13]

The "generation" of which Derrida speaks is presented inside quotation marks, as if the word bore the imprint of a suspect historicism. I myself am fond of this word, and lay claim to it. And I think that this "generation"—the one that is presented in this book—really is one, notwithstanding the disparity of the actors, for what unites them is stronger than what divides them. Of course, in this ensemble there are circulating multiple subterranean filiations, where at least three generations intersect: one was born at the beginning of the century; the second during the interwar period; and the third, my own, between 1940 and 1945.

At the risk of a certain approximation, I wish to define some traits common to this "generation" that combines three generations. Whether it issues from phenomenology, or one terms it structuralist, poststructuralist, or antistructuralist, it assembles authors whose characteristic it was to have questioned the nature of the subject and to have exposed to the light what lies hidden behind the use of this noun. Rather than cling to the idea that the subject is at one moment radically free, at another entirely determined by social or linguistic structures, the thinkers of this generation preferred to doubt the very principle of such an alternation. And that is why they persisted in criticizing, sometimes very violently, the illusions of the *Aufklärung* and the *logos*, even if it meant forcing philosophy outside philosophic discourse so as to interrogate its margins and contours in light of Marx, Freud, Nietzsche, or Heidegger, even if it meant emptying literature of any romantic content and recentering it on its own literality or on the conditions of its emergence. The poets, writers, and philosophers belonging to this generation, marked by the "new novel," wrote neither novels nor "new new novels" (which would still have been novels), but literary texts that put the very notion of novelistic universe into question.

All the friends to whom Derrida's farewells were addressed, fifteen men and one woman, were witnesses to or heirs of the two great European catastrophes of the twentieth century: the Shoah and the Gulag. They were also the actors or spectators of the end of the colonial empires, the student youth revolt, and the collapse of communism.

And if each of them was confronted, at some point in his life, with the question of the genocide of the Jews, were it only in radically challenging the positions taken by Heidegger in his "Rectoral discourse,"[14] none of them really took part in the anti-Nazi struggle—militarily or politically, and to the death—as did for example Marc Bloch, Jean Cavaillès, Boris Vildé, Georges Politzer, and Yvonne Picard.[15] Some were too young, others were elsewhere.

From 1940 to 1941 Barthes was teaching literature in two Parisian high schools. A year later, suffering from a recurrence of his tuberculosis, he found himself forced to stay in various sanatoriums for the next five years. Having collaborated in the writing of at least two texts of an anti-Semitic nature in Belgian newspapers, Paul de Man protested against the German takeover of the newspaper *Le Soir* and went to work in a publishing house.[16] Called up by the French army, Althusser and Lévinas spent the war in prison camp, while Edmond Jabès combated fascism by founding the League against anti-Semitism and the French Friendship Group at Cairo. Too young to take part, Gilles Deleuze witnessed the arrest of his brother, who would be exterminated in Auschwitz for having engaged in resistance, as was the father of Sarah Kofman, deported in 1942 as a Jew after having been rounded up by the Vichy police.

As for Blanchot, after passing his youth in the service of the Young Right, he wrote two of his major works under the occupation, *Thomas the Obscure* and *Aminadab*. The latter text owes its title to the biblical figure, but also to the younger brother of Emmanuel Lévinas, assassinated by the Nazis in Lithuania, who bore this name. Blanchot subsequently maintained discreet ties to the Resistance, protecting individuals on the run and friends, especially members of the Lévinas family. In June 1944 he barely escaped a Nazi death squad, an episode he related fifty years later in *The Instant of my Death*.[17]

Thus the stories of some link up to the stories of others, into a story of life and death into which are woven the bonds of *au revoir* and *adieu*, of death undergone, of death lived, of the farewell one says to him who remains, of the farewell one addresses to him who departs.

Jacques Lacan was not among those to whom Derrida bid farewell in *The Work of Mourning*. First, because they were never friends, and second because no family member had invited him to the cemetery before the tomb of the master, who was buried in strictest privacy in 1981, according to the consecrated formula: without honors or flowers, or speeches, or a cortège.

And yet, on another occasion Derrida had in fact included Lacan in the list of *his* dead, the list of those whose death he would have wished to celebrate: "There was death between us, it was a question of death above all," he wrote in 1990. "I would even say *only* of the death of one of us, as *with* or *chez* all those who love reciprocally. Or rather he spoke of it by himself, for I for my part never uttered a word. He spoke, by himself, of our death, of his own that would not fail to arrive, and of the death or rather of the dead man which according to him I was playing."[18]

For love of Lacan, Derrida here records a scene—a *scene of the father and death*, one could say—a scene he had told me about five years earlier and that I had related in volume 2 of my *History of Psychoanalysis in France*. Lacan had accused Derrida of "not recognizing the impasse he himself attempts on the Other by playing the dead man." A celebrated scene, overarchived by now. For love of Lacan, for the death of Lacan, for the death Lacan addresses to his recipient, for the undelivered letter that the recipient sends back, Derrida exhumes in this scene a whole secret zone of the history of his relations with Lacan. Promise of life and struggle to the death. He who remains in life dispatches his salute to the dead one, even if he be the very one who had wished most strongly that he not remain in life. The scene plays out on a deathly shore on which four characters fetch up: the king, the queen, the minister, and the chevalier, all portrayed to the life, as in a tragedy of Shakespeare, at four moments of their history, during which each attempts to exercise undivided sovereignty over the other.

Here words are not lacking, breathing is not cut short. This is clearly a true funeral oration, classic, constructed, ordered. And on this account, no doubt, it could not figure among the farewells delivered to his friends. For in this game of life and death, which had once set the two men against each other, the friend was not a friend but the adversary to whom it was necessary, now, to render posthumous homage.

The death of which Derrida speaks in dedicating, to his friends, the farewells of one who must live to bear witness that the friendship had indeed existed, is thus not of the same nature as the death of the adversary honored in retrospect. But no more is it like the heroic death of those who "died on the field of honor."

More even than soldiers who fall in battle, the committed and the resisters choose a manner of dying. They *decide* to die in saying farewell to the world in which they have lived so that a new world may come about. Thus they give their lives without ever having the certainty that their death will have been the crowning moment of a fulfilled existence. Acceptance of death coincides with the gift of life because death becomes more desirable than slavery, and freedom more desired than life. Those dead—assassinated, tortured, executed, cut to pieces, burned to ashes, thrown in trenches, annihilated, disappeared—are never allowed to have farewells spoken at the instant of their death. They have no military cemetery. No more, for that matter, than the victims of the final solution do. Their death is a crime against death.

But the farewells to those dead, to those who died for freedom, to those who died without guarantee or certainty, always come afterward. And I know of nothing more moving in this domain than the famous last words of the funeral oration for Jean Moulin delivered by André Malraux at the foot of the Pantheon on 19 December 1964: "Enter here, Jean Moulin, with your terrible cortège. With those who died in the cellars without having spoken, like you; and, what is perhaps more atrocious, having spoken; with all those wiped out and all those shorn away in the concentration camps; with the last shivering corpse of the frightful files of *Night and Fog*; fallen, finally, under crosses; with the eight thousand

Frenchwomen who did not come back from prison; with the last woman who died at Ravensbrück for having given shelter to one of ours. Enter, with the people born of shadow and vanished with shadow—our brothers in the order of the night."

Likewise, I know nothing more rigorous than the farewell of Georges Canguilhem to his friend Jean Cavaillès.[19] Finally, once again, for this twentieth century, I know nothing more overpowering than the farewells to the dead gathered by Claude Lanzmann among the *Sonderkommandos*. Words carried off, stolen, extirpated in the deepest depth of being and death, conspiracy of nothingness in order to accede to a memory of death: "You know, 'to feel' out there. . . . It was very hard to feel anything at all: imagine working day and night among the dead, the cadavers, your feelings disappear, you were dead to feeling, dead to everything."[20]

When I first read Derrida's farewells to his friends, I was just finishing Alexandre Dumas's great trilogy *The Three Musketeers*.[21] Struck by the analogies existing between these two texts, between two ways of celebrating death and saying farewell, and since I could already see that he considered himself as a survivor living on borrowed time, as the survivor who was going to die in his turn of the illness with which he was afflicted and against which he struggled, knowing all the while that he would not recover,[22] I decided to offer Jacques Derrida the story of the thirty-five years of friendship of the most celebrated heroes of French literature: Athos, Porthos, Aramis, and d'Artagnan.

In the France of the age before Colbert that Dumas chose to bring back to life, with the bourgeois cynicism he found repugnant growing ever more prevalent, the four friends incarnate a chivalric ideal that is continually ground down during their lifetimes. They have chosen pure heroism, a true challenge thrown at the new state order created by Richelieu and then Mazarin, and finally by Louis XIV with the imposition of absolutism. Every day they engage in duels, every day they kill and risk being killed. With sword in hand, and at close quarters, far from the theater of war, they never combat the contemptible, odious *enemy*, but the *adversary*, the one like them, the alter ego. For only he who is willing to risk his life for the pleasure of glory, for the splendor of panache, or for the love of a prince, conceived as the ideal of an imaginary royal lordship, only he has the right to die by being run through: the last flowering of heroic life.

Which of the four friends will depart first? Which of the four will say farewell to the other? This is the great question posed by the novel, and this is also the uncertainty that assails each of them for thirty-five years: Porthos, the giant, the naif, the baroque, the bravest of all; Athos, the melancholic and puritan noble, attached to the chivalric ideal of a past age; Aramis, the libertine, billowing and feminine, a future general of the Jesuits, secretive and cunning, but most faithful of the faithful to the only prince he has chosen for his master (Fouquet); d'Artagnan, finally, the most intelligent, most modern, most complex, in his quest for a principle of sovereignty that constantly eludes him. The friendship that unites these four men, to life and to death, and often two by two, excludes love and sexual difference. No woman would be able to share the life of any of them without putting in danger the pact that commands the very existence of the friendship.

This is why the female characters brought into the story by Dumas are devilish (Milady de Winter, the Duchess of Chevreuse), angelic (Constance Bonacieux), or deceptive (Louise de la Vallière, Anne of Austria). Whatever their role, all the women who cross the paths of the four friends are destined to destroy them. For the Musketeers are united only by the exclusive bonds of a friendship that bars each of them from being a husband, a lover, a father. And when Athos inherits a son (Bragelonne) conceived out of wedlock with the mistress of Aramis, this son, destined to perish, will have not *one* father nor *one* mother but four fathers, to the point of existing only after he has incorporated the essential element of each of them: the bravery of the first, the melancholy of the second, the femininity of the third, and the thirst for glory of the fourth.

So they had to be made to die, otherwise Dumas would have been condemned never to finish his novel, adding a fresh episode to the previous one year after year. Bound to the earth by his simplicity of spirit, Porthos departs first, crushed by rocks deep in a cave after a Herculean battle against a troop of adversaries. Aerial, and saddened by the death of his son, Athos disappears second, drawn upward by an angel who carries him off to the celestial home of interminable mourning. D'Artagnan finally, the lord of fire and war, dies third, riven by a cannon ball. And at the moment of the last passage, on which the trilogy concludes, he utters a few "cabalistic" words "that had once represented so many things on earth and that no one except this dying man understood: —Athos, Porthos, *au revoir*—Aramis, *adieu* forever!"[23]

A stunning inversion of the logic of farewell. D'Artagnan, *from his death*, and from a *time past* unknown to the living, from a time immemorial before his death, says *au revoir* to his dead friends and *adieu* forever to the friend who does not die, to the friend whose soul has already been claimed by God, to the friend who is condemned to live eternally knowing that no friend will ever bid farewell to him.

NOTES

Introduction: In Defense of Critical Thought

1. See Roudinesco, "La mémoire salie de Salvador Allende."

1. Georges Canguilhem: A Philosophy of Heroism

1. Foucault, "La vie, l'expérience, et la science" (1985), in *Dits et écrits*, 4:263–776. In 1978 Michel Foucault had drafted an earlier version of this article as a preface for the American edition of *The Normal and the Pathological*; see *Dits et écrits*, 3:429–42. The second version was initially published posthumously in *Revue de Métaphysique et de Morale* 1 (January–March 1985), a special issue dedicated to Georges Canguilhem.

2. Canguilhem, *Le normal et le pathologique.*

3. Foucault, *Histoire de la folie à l'âge classique.*

4. Canguilhem, *Vie et mort de Jean Cavaillès,* 39.

5. Foucault, *Dits et écrits*, 4:586. And Granjon, *Penser avec Michel Foucault*, 28. It is incorrect, as we shall see in the next chapter, to say that Sartre did nothing during the occupation.

6. Throughout this portion of this chapter, I take my sources from Sirinelli, *Génération intellectuelle*. See also Canguilhem, *A Vital Rationalist*. I draw as well upon the numerous notes I made from my interviews with Georges Canguilhem. My great thanks to Jean Svalgeski who put all his knowledge at my disposal. Thanks likewise to Fethi Benslama for help and pertinent comments.

7. See Sirinelli, *Génération intellectuelle*, 327, 343.

8. See "Discours prononcé par Georges Canguilhem à la distribution des prix du lycée de Charleville," 12 July 1930, and "Documents des *Libres propos*" (1932), cited by Jean-François Sirinelli, *Génération intellectuelle*, 595–96.

9. See Sirinelli, *Intellectuels et passions françaises*.

10. See Piquemal, "G. Canguilhem, professeur de terminale," 63–83.

11. Cabanis, *Les profondes années*. See also Péquignot, "Georges Canguilhem et la médicine," 39–51.

12. Edmund Husserl, *Méditations cartésiennes* (Paris: Vrin, 1986).

13. Edmund Husserl, *La crise des sciences européennes et la phénoménologie transcendantale* (Paris: Gallimard 1976).

14. On this point, readers may consult Badiou, "Y a-t-il une théorie du sujet chez Georges Canguilhem?" 295–305.

15. See Canguilhem, "Descartes et la technique," 77–85. And Canguilhem, "Activité technique et création," 81–86. See further the testimony of Piquemal, "G. Canguilhem, professeur de terminale."

16. Georges Canguilhem and Camille Planet, *Traité de logique et de morale* (Marseille: Imprimerie Robert et fils, 1939), cited by Sirinelli, *Génération intellectuelle*, 598.

17. Canguilhem, *Vie et mort de Jean Cavaillès*, 18.

18. Statement made to Jean-François Sirinelli; see Sirinelli, *Génération intellectuelle*, 598. Georges Canguilhem related the same version to me, adding repeatedly, "I did not pass my agrégation in philosophy in order to serve Marshal Pétain." See also Canguilhem's interview with François Bing in *Actualité* (Paris: Institut Synthélabo, 1998), dir. Georges Canguilhem.

19. Henry Ingrand was also a medical doctor.

20. Canguilhem tells François Bing in a humourous tone that he only practiced medicine "for a few weeks in the Maquis in the Auvergne." The facts are quite different: Canguilhem really was a genuine doctor in the Maquis.

21. In *La mort volontaire au Japon* (Paris: Gallimard, 1984), Maurice Pinguet distinguishes clearly between heroic suicide (the Japanese generals in 1945)

that allows a new society to be born, and fanatical suicide (that of Hitler and his stooges) that aims to abolish history by wiping out its traces and denying both the past and the future.

22. Chauvy, *Aubrac*.

23. No doubt this concept is universal, for we discover it in many other aristocratic societies, especially among the Japanese.

24. Vernant, *La traversée des frontières*, 60. Once he has arrived in the kingdom of the dead, Achilles is no longer the same. In the *Odyssey*, when questioned by Odysseus, he replies that he would prefer to be the lowest of slaves in life rather than Achilles in death (Vernant, *La traversée des frontières*, 80).

25. See Canguilhem, *Vie et mort de Jean Cavaillès*, 34.

26. Intervention at the meeting on the theme "être français aujourd'hui," *Le Croquant* 23 (Spring–Summer 1998), 13.

27. These words were written by René Char in the heat of action in 1943. See Char, *Feuillets d'hypnos*.

28. Canguilhem, *Le normal et le pathologique*, 9.

29. Lacan, *De la psychose paranoïaque*.

30. K. Goldstein, *La structure de l'organisme*.

31. Canguilhem, *Le normal et le pathologique*, 69.

32. Canguilhem, *Le normal et le pathologique*, 156. See also Canguilhem, "Une pédagogie de la guérison est-elle possible?" 13–26.

33. Canguilhem, *Le normal et le pathologique*, 87.

34. See Canguilhem, "La monstruosité et le monstrueux."

35. Canguilhem, *Le normal et le pathologique*, 156.

36. See Macherey, "De Canguilhem à Canguilhem en passant par Foucault," 288.

37. Canguilhem, *Le normal et le pathologique*, 156.

38. See Macherey, "La philosophie de la science de Georges Canguilhem," 50–74.

39. See Roudinesco, *Histoire de la psychanalyse en France*, 2:204.

40. See Canguilhem, "Ouverture," 40. This was the opening address, delivered on 23 November 1991, of the ninth colloquy of the Société internationale d'histoire de la psychiatrie et de la psychanalyse. The meeting was dedicated to the thirtieth anniversary of the publication of Foucault's *History of Madness*, and among the participants was Jacques Derrida. For more on this, see chap. 3.

41. See Sirinelli, *Génération intellectuelle*, 599.

42. Canguilhem, *La formation du concept de réflexe aux XVIIe et XVIIIe siècles*.

43. Saint-Sernin, "Georges Canguilhem à la Sorbonne," 91.

44. The four editions were (1) *Essai sur quelques problèmes concernant le normal et le pathologique*, Publications de la faculté des lettres de Strasbourg, Fascicule 100 (Clermont-Ferrand: 1943); (2) *Essai sur quelques problèmes concernant le normal et le pathologique*, with a preface (Paris: Les Belles Lettres, 1950); (3) *Le normal et le pathologique* (Paris: PUF, 1966); (4) *Le normal et le pathologique*, with an addendum (Paris: PUF, 1972).

45. On the heroism of the Musketeers, see chap. 6.

46. Foucault, *Naissance de la clinique*. This work appeared in the series Galien, then directed by Canguilhem.

47. For a discussion of Foucault's *History of Madness*, see chap. 3.

48. Deleuze, *Foucault*, 102.

49. Canguilhem, *Le Normal et le Pathologique*, 216. See also Macherey, "De Canguilhem à Canguilhem en passant par Foucault," 288–89.

50. Sigmund Freud, *Au-delà du principe de plaisir* (1920; *Oeuvres complètes* vol. 15 [Paris: PUF, 1996]), 273–339.

51. See especially the article "Vie," which Canguilhem wrote for the *Encylopedia universalis*.

52. See Canguilhem "Ouverture," 41.

53. Canguilhem, "Qu'est-ce que la psychologie?"

54. Canguilhem, "Qu'est-ce que la psychologie?" 381.

55. Whether of the behavioralist [*behavioriste*] or cognitive-behavioral [*cognitivo-comportementale*] variety, this psychology always aims to reduce the human subject to the sum of her behaviors and to assess them using putatively "scientific" procedures that are inadequate to their object. See Marie-José del Volgo and Roland Gori, *La santé totalitaire: Essai sur la médicalisation de l'existence* (Paris: Denoël, 2005). Behavioralism in the narrow sense is a current in psychology that was popular in the United States until 1950. It rests on the idea that human behavior is governed exclusively by the stimulus-response principle. Behavioralism in this narrow sense is thus a variant of behavioralism in the wider sense, for which the French word is *comportementalisme*. [I have slightly adapted the wording of the author's note in order to bring out the distinction she makes between behavioralism and *comportementalisme*, because English uses the word "behavioralism" indifferently for both. WM]

56. Canguilhem, "Qu'est-ce que la psychologie?" 376–77.

57. *Les Cahiers pour L'Analyse* 2 (March–April 1966).

58. Roudinesco, *Histoire de la psychanalyse en France*, vol. 2.

59. For more on Foucault, see chap. 3.

60. "For me Lacanism remains, for reasons both chronological and profession-al, a power capable of intruding on philosophy thanks to its alliance with Althusserism. Its achievements have fallen short of its ambitions, which were not, after all, illegitimate in themselves." Georges Canguilhem, private correspondence with the author, 28 September 1993.

61. For more on Sartre, see chap. 2.

62. Of whom I was one, before I became acquainted with him personally.

63. Canguilhem, "Le cerveau et la pensée," 11–33.

64. Cognitive psychology (or cognitivism; in French, *cognitivisme*) is a mythology of the brain resting on the idea of a possible equivalence between the brain and thought, itself grounded in the analogy between the cerebral function and computer technology. An offshoot of this theory known as bevavioral and cognitive therapy consists of a mixture of body drills, techniques of persuasion, and conditioning of the conscience.

65. Canguilhem, "Le cerveau et la pensée," 24.

66. Johan de Witt, the grand pensionary or chief minister of Holland, was assassinated by Orangist rioters at The Hague in 1672.

67. Canguilhem, "Le cerveau et la pensée," 32.

68. For a critique of these conceptions, see Catherine Vidal and Dorothée Ben-oit-Browaeys, *Cerveau, sexe et pouvoir*, with a preface by Maurice Godelier (Paris: Belin, 2005).

69. Georges Canguilhem, private correspondence with the author, 7 October 1988.

2. Jean-Paul Sartre: Psychoanalysis on the Shadowy Banks of the Danube

1. Sartre, *La nausée*.

2. Sartre, *Carnets de la drôle de guerre*, 100.

3. Cited by Winock, "Sartre s'est-il toujours trompé?" 35.

4. Beauvoir, *La force de l'âge*, 654.

5. Sartre, "La République du silence," 11.

6. Cited by Jean Lacouture, *De Gaulle*, vol. 1, *Le rebelle* (Paris: Seuil, 1984), 833.

7. Sartre, *L'être et le néant*. This chapter owes much to the exchanges I had

with Michel Favart during the preparation of his film *Sartre contre Sartre ou le philosophe de l'autoanalyse.*

8. Notably: *L'interprétation du rêve* (1900; *Oeuvres complètes* vol. 4, Paris: PUF, 2003); *Psychopathologie de la vie quotidienne* (1901; Paris: Gallimard, 1997); *Sur la psychanalyse: Cinq conférences* (1910; Paris: Gallimard, 1991); *Conférences d'introduction à la psychanalyse* (1916–17; Paris: Gallimard, 1999); *Métapsychologie* (1915; *Oeuvres complètes* vol. 13, Paris: PUF, 1988); *Au-delà du principe de plaisir* (1920; *Oeuvres complètes* vol. 15, Paris: PUF, 1996); *Psychologie de masse at analyse du moi* (1921; *Oeuvres complètes* vol. 16, Paris: PUF, 1991); *Le moi et le ça* (ibid.).

9. Edmund Husserl, *La crise des sciences européennes et la phénoménologie transcendantale* (Paris: Gallimard 1976).

10. For more on Canguilhem, see chap. 1. See as well Jambet, "Y a-t-il une philosophie française?"

11. Sartre, *L'engrenage.* See Contat and Rybalka, *Les écrits de Sartre.* [*L'engrenage* means "the gears," but also "the mechanism or process that traps one." WM]

12. See Roudinesco, *Histoire de la psychanalyse en France*, vol. 2; and Roudinesco and Plon, *Dictionnaire de la psychanalyse.*

13. Louis Althusser was the first in France to call attention to the Soviet denunciation of psychoanalysis. See Althusser, "Freud et Lacan." For more on Althusser, see chap. 4.

14. Sartre, *Questions de méthode*, 56.

15. Sartre, *Questions de méthode*, 56.

16. Sartre, *L'être et le néant*, 663.

17. Cited by Contat and Rybalka in *Les écrits de Sartre*, 386.

18. *Questions de méthode* appeared initially in *Les Temps Modernes* with the title "Existentialisme et marxisme."

19. Sartre, *L'idiot de la famille.*

20. Freud founded the International Psychoanalytic Association in 1910. Notable examples of directors who immigrated to the United States include Vincente Minelli, Elia Kazan, Alfred Hitchcock, and Charlie Chaplin.

21. Hale, *Freud and the Americans.*

22. Elia Kazan, *Splendor in the Grass* (1961), with Nathalie Wood (Wilma Dean) and Warren Beatty (Bud Stamper). Charles Chaplin, *Limelight* (1952), with Chaplin (Calvero), Claire Bloom (Terry), and Geraldine, Michael, and Josephine Chaplin (the children).

23. Jean-Paul Sartre, *Huis clos* (1945; English title *No Exit*), and *Les mouches*.

24. John Huston, *Freud: The Secret Passion* (1962), with Montgomery Clift (Freud), Susanna York (Cecily Koertner), Larry Parks (Josef Breuer), Susan Kohner (Martha Freud), and Fernand Ledoux (Charcot).

25. John Huston, *An Open Book*, 295–96; in French, *John Huston*, 276–77.

26. Sartre, *Lettres au castor*, 358–60.

27. Sartre, "Entretien avec Kenneth Tynan," *Afrique Action* (10 July 1961).

28. Sigmund Freud, *La naissance de la psychanalyse* (London, 1950; expurgated ed., Paris: PUF, 1956); Josef Breuer, *Études sur l'hysterie* (Vienna 1895; Paris: PUF, 1956); Ernest Jones, *La vie et l'oeuvre de Sigmund Freud*, vol. 1 (1953; Paris: PUF, 1958).

29. Anna O.'s real name was Bertha Pappenheim (1860–1938). See Hirschmüller, *Josef Breuer*.

30. For the exact historical reconstruction of these events, see Ellenberger, *Médicines de l'âme*, and Hirschmüller, *Josef Breuer*.

31. On the career of the real Theodor Meynert (1833–92), see Ellenberger, *Médicines de l'âme*, and Sulloway, *Freud*.

32. Schneider, *Blessures de mémoire*.

33. Wilhelm Fliess, *Les relations entre le nez et les organes genitaux féminins selon leurs significations biologiques* (Vienna, 1897; Paris: Seuil, 1977).

34. Azouri, *J'ai réussi là où le paranoïaque échoue*.

35. Wilhelm Fliess (1858–1928). On the career of this colorful scientist, see Sulloway, *Freud*. See also Freud's complete correspondence with him, not yet available in French: *Briefe an Wilhelm Fliess, 1887–1904* (Frankfurt a. M.: Fischer, 1986). On Bertha Pappenheim, see Hirschmüller, *Josef Breuer*, and Ellenberger, *Histoire de la découverte de l'inconscient*.

36. Alexandre Koyré, *Études d'histoire de la pensée scientifique* (1966; Paris: Gallimard, 1973).

37. Sartre, *Le scénario Freud*.

38. Sigmund Freud, *Sigmund Freud présenté par lui-même* (Vienna, 1925; Paris: Gallimard, 1984).

39. Sartre, *Les séquestrés d'Altona*.

40. John Huston, *The Misfits* (1961), screenplay by Arthur Miller, with Marilyn Monroe (Roslyn Taber), Clark Gable (Cay Langland), Montgomery Clift (Perce Howland), and Eli Wallach (Guido).

41. Rudolph Loewenstein (1898–1976) was an American psychiatrist and psychoanalyst born in Polish Galicia, who established himself first in Paris

before leaving for the United States. With Heinz Hartmann and Ernst Kris, he was the main exponent of the ego psychology school.

42. Marilyn Monroe left her estate to her analyst for the purpose of supporting the work of the Hampstead Child Therapy Clinic in London.

43. Cited by Marie-Magdeleine Lessana, *Marilyn, portrait d'une apparition* (Paris: Bayard, 2005), 215. See also D. Spoto, *Marilyn: La biographie* (Paris: Presses de la Cité, 1993); Jean Garabé, "Marilyn Monroe et le président Schreber," *Confrontations psychiatriques* 40 (1999).

44. Sartre, *Le scénario Freud*, 355.

45. See Roudinesco, *Pourquoi la psychanalyse?*

46. Freud to Fliess, 21 September 1897 (excerpts), in Freud, *The Complete Letters*, ed. and trans. Jeffrey Moussaieff Masson, 264–66. On 11 February 1897, continuing a letter begun on 8 February, Freud had posited that certain hysterical migraines originate in the fact that the women had been forced in infancy to perform fellatio on adults in "scenes where the head is held still." It is the memory of this scene, he explains, that subsequently caused their migraines. And he adds: "Unfortunately, my own father was one of these perverts and is responsible for the hysteria of my brother (all of whose symptoms are identifications) and those of several younger sisters. The frequency of this circumstance often makes me wonder." Freud to Fliess, 11 February 1897, trans. Masson, *The Complete Letters*, 230–31. [The author cites the French translation of both letters from Masson, *Le Réel escamoté*. WM]

47. Freud's father was Jakob Freud (1815–96).

48. Sartre, *Les mots*, 11. The eminent psychoanalyst was Jean-Bertrand Pontalis.

49. Sartre, *Les mots*, 210.

50. Sartre, *Le mur*.

51. Sartre, "Autoportrait à soixante-dix ans."

52. Laing and Cooper, *Raison et violence*.

53. Sartre, "Entretien sur l'anthropologie," 87–96.

54. *Les Temps Modernes* (April 1968): 1813.

55. For more on Deleuze's *Anti-Oedipe*, see chap. 5.

56. See Roudinesco, *Jacques Lacan*. The full text of Foucault's statements can be found in Eribon, *Foucault et ses contemporaines*, 261–63.

57. Foucalt, *Dits et écrits*, vol. 1, 514.

58. Lacan, "Le temps logique et l'assertion de certitude anticipée."

3. Michel Foucault: Readings of *History of Madness*

1. Foucault, *Histoire de la folie à l'âge classique*, introduction. Foucault defended his main thesis on 20 May 1961 before an examining board composed of Henri Gouthier (president), Georges Canguilhem (first rapporteur) and Daniel Lagache (second rapporteur). On the same day he defended his subordinate thesis on Kant, with Jean Hyppolite and Maurice de Gandillac as rapporteurs. When offered to Gallimard, the work was turned down by Brice Parain, despite the favorable opinion of Roger Caillois. Instead it was published in the autumn by Plon, at the instance of Philippe Ariès and with the title *Folie et déraison, histoire de la folie à l'âge classique*. This first edition, now out of print, comprised a short preface, which Michel Foucault cut from the 1972 edition. See Foucalt, *Dits et écrits*, 1:159–67. Foucault also changed the title at that time. The 1972 Gallimard edition—the one referenced throughout this book—comprises a new preface in which Foucault explains why he has chosen not to update his book to take into account current events: he had at first intended to add a discussion of the antipsychiatry movement, but had then decided not to. The 1972 edition also includes an appendix containing two important texts: a response to Henri Gouhier and another to Jacques Derrida.

2. Henri Ey (1900–1977), French psychiatrist. He was editor in chief of the journal *L'évolution psychiatrique* and the inventor of an approach to mental illness labeled *organo-dynamique*. It was based on the work of the English neurologist John Hughlings Jackson (1835–1911), who regarded the psychical functions not as something static, but rather as dependent upon one another, in descending order.

3. Lacan, *De la psychose paranoïaque dans ses rapports avec la personnalité*.

4. [The author has cited this famous passage from Descartes without a note, which her French readers would not have required. It is found in *Méditations* 1.4. She uses the standard French translation of de Luynes (1647; Descartes wrote the work in Latin). The English translation in the text is mine. *Mais quoi!* is an untranslatable interjection expressing remonstration. WM]

5. Lacan, "Le stade du miroir comme formateur de la fonction du Je," 93–101.

6. *L'Évolution Psychiatrique*, vol.1, no. 2, 226.

7. See Surya, *Georges Bataille*.

8. This pious history is best illustrated in René Semelaigne, *Les pionniers*, from which these lines are taken.

9. "Rapport de Georges Canguilhem du 19 avril 1960" in Eribon, *Michel Foucault*. See as well Canguilhem, "Sur l'*Histoire de la folie* en tant que événement;" Canguilhem, Présentation; Canguilhem, "Mort de l'homme ou épuisement du cogito?"

10. All these points of view were expressed during the colloquy in Toulouse by, among others, Georges Daumezon, Henri Sztulman, Antoine Porot, Eugène Minkowski, and Julien Rouart. See further Castel, "Les aventures de la pratique."

11. During the ninth colloquy of the Société internationale d'histoire de la psychiatrie et de la psychanalyse on 23 November 1991, which I organized, Claude Quétel delivered a harangue for the prosecution against Foucault in the presence of all the other participants: Georges Canguilhem, Jacques Derrida, Arlette Farge, Jacques Postel, François Bing, René Major, Agostino Pirella, Pierre Macherey. See *Penser la folie*.

12. Though he had to leave Warsaw in a hurry because of a liaison in which he engaged with a young man who was a police informer, Foucault had been happy there in 1958–59 in his role as cultural adviser. See Eribon, *Michel Foucault et ses contemporaines*, 112.

13. Michel Foucault, letter to Jacqueline Verdeaux, 19 August 1954, cited by Eribon, *Michel Foucault et ses contemporaines*, 116. Foucault used to amuse his friends by saying that he would one day hold a "chair in madness" at the Collège de France (105).

14. Althusser, *L'avenir dure longtemps*. This work is discussed at length in chap. 4.

15. Eribon, *Michel Foucault et ses contemporaines*, 121–22.

16. Foucault, *Maladie mentale et psychologie*.

17. Pierre Macherey was the first to point out that Foucault had not only changed his conception of madness between 1954 and 1961, but had also changed the text of his 1954 study of mental illness to make it conform to his new conception when it was republished in 1962. See Macherey, "Aux sources de l'*Histoire de la folie*."

18. In an article full of praise, Roland Barthes did nevertheless locate *History of Madness* in the Annales tradition, claiming that Lucien Febvre would have liked this "audacious book which renders to history a fragment of nature, and transforms what until now we took for a medical fact into a fact of civilization." Barthes, "De part et d'autre," 168.

19. Swain, *Le sujet de la folie*, prefaced by Marcel Gauchet, "De Pinel à Freud." The first to focus on deconstructing the myth of abolition was in fact Jacques Postel, whose seminar Gladys Swain had attended. See Postel, *Genèse de la psychiatrie*.

20. Gauchet and Swain, *La pratique de l'esprit humain*.

21. Foucault, *La volonté de savoir*.

22. See Furet, *Le passé d'une illusion*. In this book, farced with errors and hasty judgments, Foucault and Althusser are treated with contempt and ignorance, and laid under suspicion of having qualified the bourgeois order as "totalitarian." As for their "heirs," with whom the author is unacquainted, they are quite simply insulted: "The former 1968ers quickly made their peace with the market, advertising, and the consumer society, in which they often swim like fish in water, as if they had only denounced its faults so as to adapt to it better. But they are determined to preserve the intellectual benefits of the idea of revolution while establishing themselves socially. In their favorite authors, Marcuse, Foucault and Althusser, totalitarianism is an exclusive feature of the bourgeois order. You would search their works in vain for a critical analysis of 'real socialism' in the twentieth century" (563). I note that Foucault did not express a negative opinion of Furet's book *Penser la révolution française* (Paris: Gallimard, 1978). On the shifts in Furet's interpretation of the French Revolution, see Olivier Bétourne and Aglaia I. Hartig, *Penser l'histoire de la Révolution: Deux siècles de passion française* (Paris: La Découverte, 1989).

23. Gilles Deleuze and Félix Guattari, *Capitalisme et schizophrenie*, vol. 1, *L'anti-Oedipe* (Paris: Minuit, 1972). For more on this, see chap. 5.

24. Foucault, *La volonté de savoir*, 198.

25. On this question, see Major, *De l'élection,* and Roudinesco and Plon, *Dictionnaire de la psychanalyse*.

26. Swain, "Chimie, cerveau, esprit: Paradoxes épistémologiques des psychotropes en médecine mentale," preceded by "À la recherche d'une autre histoire de la folie" (Paris: Gallimard, 1994), 263–79. In his introduction to this collection of Gladys Swain's writings, Marcel Gauchet cites with approval the "dazzling merit" and "oracular obscurity" of Lacan, while blaming Deleuze and Guattari for what he too calls their "Nietzschean-Heideggerianism."

27. Ferry and Renaut, *La pensée 68*. For comment on this book, see Derrida and Roudinesco, *De quoi demain*.

28. A notable example is Alain Ehrenburg; see "Les guerres du sujet" and "Le

sujet cérébral," *Esprit* (November 2004): 84–85. And in the same issue, Pierre-Henri Castel, "Psychothérapies: Quelle évaluation?"

29. Foucault, *Les anormaux*, 13. Foucault is speaking here of experts in criminology.

30. Among historians, Michelle Perrot is the author of one of the finest analyses of Foucault's texts on the penal system and the punishment meted out to delinquents and the marginalized; see Perrot, *Les ombres de l'histoire: Crime et châtiment au XIXe siècle* (Paris: Flammarion, 2001). See as well Paul Veyne, "Foucault révolutionne l'histoire," in *Comment on écrit l'histoire* (Paris: Seuil, 1978) On the considerable impact of Foucault's work on the study of sexuality, see Eribon, *Michel Foucault et ses contemporaines.*

31. J. Goldstein, *Console and Classify.*

32. The word *psychiatrie* appeared in 1802, taking the place of *alienisme.*

33. For more on article 64 of the penal code, see chap. 4.

34. Louis Althusser was judged "not responsible" for the murder of his wife by virtue of article 64 of the penal code. It was in order to assume this responsibility that he wrote his autobiography. For more on this, see chap. 4.

35. See Michel Foucault, "À quoi rêvent les Iraniens?" in *Dits et écrits*, 3:688–94. Accused first by Pierre Debray-Ritzen, an adept of the New Right and a great adversary of Freudianism, then by Pierre and Claude Broyelle, one-time admirers of the Chinese Cultural Revolution, Foucault replied in the newspaper *Le Monde* for 11–12 May 1979: "An astonishing superimposition, it was able to bring about, in the middle of the twentieth century, a movement strong enough to overturn a regime seemingly among the best-armed, while being close to old dreams that the Occident knew in the past, when men attempted to inscribe the figures of spirituality on the ground of politics. . . . My theoretical morality is antistrategic: to be respectful when a singularity occurs, but intransigent as soon as power infringes on the universal" (*Dits et écrits*, 3:793–94). See, too, Foucault's interview with Pierre Blanchet and Claire Brière (*Dits et écrits*, 3:743–55); and Afary and Anderson, *Foucault and the Iranian Revolution.*

36. On this, see the excellent work of Dreyfus and Rabinow, *Michel Foucault.*

37. [In English in the original; glossed in the note as *sexualité sans risque.* WM]

38. See Mirko D. Grmek, *Histoire du sida: Début et origine d'une pandémie actuelle* (Paris: Payot, 1989).

39. Eribon, *Michel Foucault*, 348.

40. Miller, *The Passion of Michel Foucault*. The book was a best seller in the United States.

41. I have denounced conditioning therapies grounded in the violation of conscience in *Pourquoi la psychanalyse?*

42. Guibert, "Les secrets d'un homme," and *À l'ami qui ne m'a pas sauvé la vie*.

43. It was from the same perspective that Foucault's numerous "errors" concerning the case of Pierre Rivière were cataloged. See Foucault, *Moi, Pierre Rivière, ayant égorgé ma mère, ma soeur et mon frère*. Once again, this was less about criticizing debatable methods and interpretations than it was about accusing the philosopher and his team of justifying the crime: "They are unwilling and unable to follow the reversal of power they sketch to its conclusion, in other words justification of the crime. They take up a stance of submissive admiration that renders the memory of Pierre Rivière taboo, almost ineffable." Philippe Lejeune, "Lire Pierre Rivière," *Le Débat* 66 (October 1991), 95.

44. Included in Derrida, *L'écriture et la différence*.

45. Dosse, *Histoire du structuralisme*.

46. Eribon, *Michel Foucault*, 147.

47. On the manner in which Derrida paid homage to Foucault after his death, see chap. 6.

48. Foucault, *Les mots et les choses*. The title of the published English translation is *The Order of Things*.

49. As Gilles Deleuze revealed in *Foucault*, 11.

50. Sartre, *L'existentialisme est un humanisme*.

51. *Les Temps Modernes* (November 1946–July 1947).

52. This is how Ian Kershaw defined the *Führerprinzip* in his monumental work *Hitler*, 2 vols. (New York: Norton, 1999); in French, *Hitler* (Paris: Flammarion, 2004).

53. This history is very well known today, but it continues to provoke various interpretations. See Dominique Janicaud, *Heidegger en France*, 2 vols. (Paris: Albin Michel, 2001). Emmanuel Faye alone, in a work that does in fact contain new, undeniable, and crushing information about Heidegger's Nazism, reduces his thought to a Nazi ideology. Faye goes so far as to assert that it ought no longer to be taught as philosophy, and that the deconstructionists and other antihumanists—from Foucault to Althusser, by way of Derrida and the American university professors who adhere to this

school—are no more than adepts of Heideggerian *Destruktion*. See Emmanuel Faye, *Heidegger: L'introduction du nazisme dans la philosophie* (Paris: Albin Michel, 2005), 514–15. On the relations between Jean Beaufret, Heidegger, and Lacan, see Roudinesco, *Jacques Lacan*.

54. Martin Heidegger, *Lettre sur l'humanisme* (Paris: Aubier, 1957).

55. Lévi-Strauss quoted in Eribon, *De près ou de loin*, 225–26.

56. I return to the idea of everyday, nondescript fascism in chap. 5.

57. Martin Jay, *The Dialectical Imagination: A History of the Frankfurt School and the Institute of Social Research, 1923–1950* (Boston: Little Brown, 1973); in French, *L'imagination dialectique: Histoire de l'école de Frankfurt, 1923–1950* (Paris: PUF, 1977).

58. Foucault, *Les mots et les choses*, 15.

59. Foucault, *Les mots et les choses*, 398.

60. Canguilhem, "Mort de l'homme ou épuisement du cogito."

4. Louis Althusser: The Murder Scene

1. Althusser, *L'avenir dure longtemps*. The title of the published English translation is *The Future Lasts Forever*.

2. Hélène Rytmann (1910–80) is also known as Hélène Legotien and Hélène Legotien-Rytmann because "Legotien" had been her cover name in the Resistance and she continued to use it. She was buried in the cemetery of Bagneux in the section reserved for Jews.

3. Article 64 stipulated that "there is neither crime nor delict when the person suspected was in a state of dementia at the time of the deed." By the law of 22 July 1992, article 64 was replaced by article 122, which stipulates: "The person who was afflicted at the moment of the deed with a psychical or neuropsychical disturbance that altered his discernment or hampered his control of his actions is not penally responsible. The person who was afflicted at the moment of the deed with a psychical or neuropsychical disturbance that altered his discernment or hampered his control of his actions remains punishable: nevertheless, the court takes this factor into account when it determines the length of the sentence and decides under what conditions it shall be served."

4. Sarraute, "Petite faim."

5. Althusser, *L'avenir dure longtemps*, 19. "Even though I was released from psychiatric confinement two years ago, I remain, for the public to whom I am known, one of the *disappeared*. Neither dead nor alive, still unburied

but 'unemployed'—Foucault's magnificent word to designate madness: *disappeared*. . . . One of the disappeared may startle public opinion by turning up again (as I am now doing) in the broad daylight of life . . . in the great sunshine of Polish freedom."

6. Althusser, *L'avenir dure longtemps*, 18.

7. I refer essentially to the coverage in *Le Monde*, *Libération*, *Le Matin*, and *Le Nouvel Observateur*.

8. Cited by Robert Maggiori, *Libération*, 18 November 1980.

9. Jamet, "Le crime du philosophe Althusser."

10. Jean Bousquet was the director of the École Normale Supérieure at this time.

11. Pierre-André Taguieff takes the prize for the greatest contemporary detestation of Louis Althusser. In a work claiming to denounce anti-Semitic hatred—and that is no more than a tissue of police-style imprecations against those who do not think like him—he endorses the view that the philosopher got special treatment after having premeditated a killing and taught his students to view crime positively, as akin to revolution. He goes on to characterize those in the philosopher's circle, and all the rebels of May 1968, as "islamo-communists," meaning Stalinist terrorists tainted with anti-Semitism: "Balibar was, after all, one of the inner circle of his master and friend Althusser, who, it should be recalled—despite attempts to hush the matter up—was interned after having assassinated his companion 'in a moment of madness' (as it was called)." Careful to exempt Althusser from anti-Semitism, Taguieff still manages to hint, through a denial, that he had suspected him of having killed Hélène because she was Jewish: "The Jewish origin of the victim seems not to have constituted a determining factor in the murder. The essential point lies elsewhere: in the postulate that killers are always excusable, or pardonable, if they have presented themselves as 'revolutionaries' or partisans of the 'good cause.'" Taguieff, *Prêcheurs de haine*, 317–18.

12. See Balibar, *Écrits pour Althusser*, 119–23.

13. See Althusser, "Sur la Révolution culturelle." This article was published by Althusser anonymously. Contrary to what has since been stated, this text, which displays great political naïveté in light of the crimes committed by the Red Guards, does not include any call for the massacre of the "enemies" of the working class, or any "racist" conception of the notion of class struggle. Althusser wrote: "In no case, even against the enemy of the bourgeois class (crimes being punished by the law), ought one to resort to

'blows' and violence, but always to reasoning and persuasion." See Marty, *Louis Althusser*, 141–45.

14. In *La pensée 68*, Ferry and Renaut state that they preferred not to devote a chapter to the oeuvre of Louis Althusser, on the grounds that "it is in the work of Bourdieu that the French Marxism of the 1960s continues to hold a place in the intellectual field. Althusserism, even in Althusser's disciples, seems very dated, and irresistibly calls to mind a recent but outmoded past, like the music of the Beatles or Godard's early films" (240). As for Furet, in *Le Passé d'une illusion*, he accuses Foucault and Althusser of having depicted bourgeois society as a totalitarian system.

15. Althusser, *L'avenir dure longtemps*, 152.

16. Moulier-Boutang, *Louis Althusser*, 147ff.

17. Althusser, *Lettres à Franca*, 215.

18. I have related this episode in *Histoire de la psychanalyse en France*, vol. 2.

19. Althusser, *Journal de captivité*.

20. Althusser, *L'avenir dure longtemps*, 102.

21. Althusser, *Pour Marx*; Althusser, Balibar, Establet, Macherey, and Rancière, *Lire "Le Capital."*

22. Althusser, *Pour Marx*, 19.

23. Derrida, *Chaque fois unique*, 149.

24. Karl Marx, *Les manuscrits économico-philosophiques de 1844* in *Écrits de jeunesse*, presentation by Kostas Papaioanu (Paris: Éditions sociales, 1956); *Thèses sur Feuerbach* (Paris: Éditions sociales, 1956). Althusser, *Écrits philosophiques et politiques*.

25. Althusser, *L'avenir dure longtemps*, p. III.

26. Althusser, *L'avenir dure longtemps*, p. III. I can testify that Louis Althusser always gave the same version of what had happened.

27. Sollers, *Femmes*. In this novel Althusser is called Lutz.

28. Sollers, *Femmes*, 106–7.

29. Sollers, *Femmes*, 111.

30. Jean Guitton, "Entretien avec Pierre Boncenne," *Lire* 121 (October 1985): 126.

31. Régis Debray, *Les masques* (Paris: Gallimard, 1988).

32. The philosopher had thought of calling his testimony *Brève histoire d'un meurtrier* (Brief History of a Murderer) or *D'une nuit l'aube* (Of a Night the Dawn).

33. Althusser, *L'avenir dure longtemps*, 273. André Malraux, *Antimémoires* (Par-

is: Gallimard, 1967), 1:155. Éric Marty gives an interpretation of this title that differs from mine. See Marty, *Louis Althusser*, 43.

34. Althusser, *L'avenir dure longtemps*, 11–12.

35. Louis Althusser was known to have unusual physical strength.

36. "An early-morning massage transforming itself, without his realizing it into a strangulation, without the victim being there other than silently (as if dead), then dead for real. Without the passage from life to death being assignable. Without the consciousness present here in the writing being describable as conscious." (Moulier-Boutang, *Louis Althusser*, 38.) The murder took place in a room that was not normally occupied either by Louis or by his companion. No one knows the reason why Hélène had chosen to sleep there on that night.

37. Althusser, *L'avenir dure longtemps*, 243.

38. In 1953 Jacques Lacan for his part had asked his brother Marc-François to arrange a meeting for him with the pope, so that he could expound his doctrine to him. In the same period he had sought a meeting with Maurice Thorez. He did indeed believe, and with good reason, that the Catholic church on one hand and the French Communist Party on the other, were the two major institutions susceptible of incorporating the Freudian doctrine. I have recounted this episode in *Histoire de la psychanalyse en France*, vol. 2. See as well Jean Guitton, *Un siècle, une vie* (Paris: Robert Laffont, 1988), 156.

39. Althusser, *L'avenir dure longtemps*, 245. We know today that Louis Althusser did not limit himself to taking the antipsychotic medication his psychiatrists prescribed for him. He also resorted, like Hélène, to constant self-medication, swallowing drugs of every sort without, for that matter, giving up the consumption of alcohol.

40. Althusser, *L'avenir dure longtemps*, 163.

41. Althusser, *L'avenir dure longtemps*, 137.

42. Moulier-Boutang, *Louis Althusser*, 344–444.

43. Althusser, *L'avenir dure longtemps*, 109 and 116.

44. Althusser, *L'avenir dure longtemps*, 154.

45. See Michel de Certeau, *La fable mystique* (Paris: Gallimard, 1982). Christian Jambet, *La grande résurrection d'Alamût: Les formes de la liberté dans le shî'isme ismaélien* (Lagrasse: Verdier, 1990). It was Certeau who first remarked to me in 1969 that Althusser's destiny resembled that of the great mystics of Christianity and that his oeuvre bore traces of this.

46. This was the case of Claire Z., for example, with whom he had a long relationship before meeting Franca Madonia when he was forty-two.

47. Althusser, *Lettres à Franca*, 14.

48. On the relations between Louis Althusser and Jacques Lacan, see Althusser, *Écrits sur la psychanalyse*, and Roudinesco, *Jacques Lacan*, 383–403.

49. Georgette Althusser (1921–91), whose married name was Boddaert; in 1957 she sank into a serious depression after the birth of her son, François, who was raised by his grandparents and is today his uncle's heir and controller of his literary estate. Thanks to him the philosopher's papers were deposited and made available for consultation at the IMEC (Institut Mémoires de l'Édition Contemporaine).

50. Cited by Moulier-Boutang, *Louis Althusser*, 75–76. This text, obtained by Fernando Navarro in 1984, was published in Spanish in 1990. Althusser had refused to have it appear in print while he was alive.

51. Louis Althusser, letter of 18 July 1966, in Althusser, *Écrits sur la psychanalyse*.

52. Althusser, *Lettres à Franca*, 771.

53. Althusser, *Lettres à Franca*, 806. Franca met Louis Althusser once more, at Bologna in 1980. She died in Paris from the effects of cirrhosis of the liver caused by hepatitis C, without having been able to visit him after he was interned in the Saint-Anne hospital following the murder of Hélène.

54. Daniel Paul Schreber, *Mémoires d'un névropathe* (Leipzig 1903; Paris: Seuil, 1975). Sigmund Freud, "Remarques psychanalytiques sur l'autobiographie d'un cas de paranoïa" (1911) in *Cinq psychanalyses* (Paris: PUF, 1954), 263–321.

55. Daniel Sibony, *Libération*, 22 June 1992, reprinted in Sibony, *Le peuple psy* (Paris: Balland, 1993).

56. Lemoine-Luccioni, *L'histoire à l'envers*, 8.

57. Bénézech and Lacoste, "L'uxoricide de Louis Althusser selon son récit autobiographique."

58. Green, "Analyse d'une vie tourmentée," 31.

59. Green, "Analyse d'une vie tourmentée," 31.

60. Allouch, *Louis Althusser*, 51.

61. *Louis du néant*, by Gérard Pommier, recounts the melancholic itinerary of the philosopher. It is largely based on the work of Yann Moulier-Boutang and adds nothing new to Althusser's autobiography.

62. In his first autobiography, *Les faits* (1976), Althusser had already adopted this pose. Éric Marty takes it at face value and makes Althusser into a real

impostor, responsible "for a million dead" (the Chinese executed during the Cultural Revolution). See Marty, *Louis Althusser*, 141.

63. Althusser, *L'avenir dure longtemps*, 211.

64. The decision was taken by Georges Marchais during the twenty-second congress of the Parti Communiste Français in February 1976. The dictatorship of the proletariat can be defined as "the ensemble of temporary political measures that the proletariat must take in order to prevail during the revolutionary crisis, and so resolve it." It is part of an exceptional situation and has a practical purpose. See Georges Labica and Gérard Bensussan, *Dictionnaire critique du marxisme* (Paris: PUF, 1982) and Étienne Balibar, *Sur la dictature du prolétariat* (Paris: Maspero, 1976).

65. Derrida, *Spectres de Marx*, 12.

66. Derrida, *Spectres de Marx*, 141.

5. Gilles Deleuze: Anti-Oedipal Variations

1. Foucault, *Dits et écrits*, 2:75. Deleuze, *Différence et répétition*; Deleuze, *Logique du sens*.

2. Gilles Deleuze taught philosophy for forty years. See *L'abécédaire de Gilles Deleuze*, an eight-hour film with Claire Parnet, made by Pierre-André Boutang (Éditions Montparnasse).

3. Deleuze and Guattari, *Capitalisme et schizophrenie*, vol. 1, *L'anti-Oedipe*, and vol. 2, *Mille plateaux*. Minuit published an augmented edition of *L'anti-Oedipe* in 1992, and republished both volumes of *Capitalisme et schizophrenie* in 2004.

4. Deleuze, *Pourparlers*.

5. Deleuze, *Pourparlers*, 15.

6. Derrida, *Chaque fois unique*, 236.

7. Bernard-Henri Lévy, *La barbarie à visage humain* (Paris: Grasset, 1977).

8. Gilles Deleuze, "Le Juif riche" (18 February 1977), in *Deux régimes de fous*, 122–26. The film was *L'ombre des anges*, directed by Daniel Schmid from a screenplay by Rainer Werner Fassbinder. Following the ban, a group of fifty personalities signed a petition "standing up against the irresponsibility that consists in not analyzing the structure of a film" and "against the acts of violence that prohibit a film from being seen."

9. Deleuze, *L'abécédaire*; and "Huit ans après: Entretien avec Catherine Clément" in *Deux régimes de fous*, 165.

10. Deleuze, "Il a été mon maître," in *L'île déserte et autres textes*, 113.

11. Eribon, *Sur cet instant fragile*, 186–87. See as well Didier Eribon, *Réflexions sur la question gay* (Paris: Fayard, 1999), and *Une morale minoritaire: Variations sur un thème de Jean Genet* (Paris: Fayard, 2001).

12. See Jean-Claude Milner, *La politique des choses* (Paris: Navarin, 2005).

13. Deleuze and Guattari, *Mille plateaux*; "Huit ans après: Entretien avec Catherine Clément," in *Deux régimes de fous*, 162–66.

14. Deleuze, *Logique du sens*, 306.

15. Patrice Maniglier and David Rabouin, "Quelle politique?" *Magazine Littéraire* 406 (February 2002): 53. The stance of Toni Negri and Michael Hardt belongs in this tradition; see their book *Empire* (Cambridge, Mass.: Harvard University Press, 2000); in French, *Empire* (Paris: Exils, 2001).

16. See Streicher, "À propos de *Différence et répétition*."

17. Guattari, *Écrits pour L'anti-Oedipe*.

18. On the necessity of rediscovering the tragic character of the Freudian Oedipus in order to "depsycholgize" it, see Roudinesco, *La famille en désordre*.

19. It is in *Pourparlers* that Gilles Deleuze and Félix Guattari discuss *L'anti-Oedipe* and *Mille plateaux* most fully, especially in their interviews with Robert Maggiori and Didier Eribon.

20. "Yes, Deleuze was our great physicist, he contemplated the fire of the stars for us, sounded chaos, took the measure of organic life. . . . He was the one who could not bear the idea that 'great Pan is dead.'" Badiou, *Deleuze* (Paris: Hachette, 1997), 150.

21. Foucault, "Préface à l'édition américaine de *L'anti-Oedipe*," *Dits et écrits*, 3:134.

6. Jacques Derrida: The Moment of Death

1. Derrida, *Chaque fois unique*. The book comprises Derrida's farewells to Roland Barthes, Paul de Man, Michel Foucault, Max Loreau, Jean-Marie-Benoist, Louis Althusser, Edmond Jabès, Joseph N. Riddel, Michel Servière, Louis Marin, Sarah Kofman, Gilles Deleuze, Emmanuel Lévinas, Jean-François Lyotard, Gérard Granel, and Maurice Blanchot. See as well, on the death of Hans-Georg Gadamer, Derrida, *Béliers*.

2. See Derrida and Roudinesco, *De quoi demain*.

3. Derrida, *Béliers*, 20.

4. Élisabeth Young-Bruehl, *Anna Freud* (1988; Paris, Payot, 1991).

5.   Sigmund Freud and Ludwig Binswanger, *Correspondance, 1908–1938* (Paris: Calmann-Lévy, 1995).

6.   This is the reason Jocasta kills herself before the self-mutilation of Oedipus in Sophocles' play.

7.   See Michel Vovelle, *La mort et l'Occident* (1983; Paris: Gallimard, 2000).

8.   Derrida, *Chaque fois unique*, 252.

9.   Derrida, *Chaque fois unique*, 137.

10. Simone de Beauvoir, *La cérémonie des adieux* (Paris: Gallimard, 1981).

11. Charles Baudelaire, Marcel Proust, Victor Hugo.

12. Excellent short biobibliographies prepared by Kas Saghafi have been added to *Chaque fois unique*. They shed historical light on the farewells.

13. Derrida, *Chaque fois unique*, 236.

14. Martin Heidegger, *Auto-affirmation de l'université allemande*, German text with French translation by Gérard Granel (Toulouse: TER, 1982).

15. See *La Liberté de l'Esprit: Visages de la Résistance* 16 (autumn 1987).

16. On this matter, see Derrida, *Mémoires pour Paul de Man*.

17. Maurice Blanchot, *Thomas l'obscur* (Paris: Gallimard, 1941); *Aminadab* (Paris: Gallimard, 1942); *L'instant de ma mort* (1994; Paris: Gallimard, 2002).

18. Derrida, *Résistances de la psychanalyse*. The lecture "Pour l'amour de Lacan," from which these lines are quoted, was delivered in May 1990 at the colloquy "Lacan avec les philosophes" organized by René Major, Philippe Lacoue-Labarthe, and Patrick Guyomard in the setting of the Collège Internationale de Philosophie.

19. On Canguilhem's farewell to Cavaillès, see chap. 1.

20. Lanzmann, *Shoah*.

21. Alexandre Dumas, *Les trois Mousquetaires, Vingt ans après,* and *Le vicomte de Bragelonne* (1844–50; Paris: Laffont, 1991 in the collection Bouquins). The second volume has an excellent preface by Dominique Fernandez, "Dumas baroque."

22. Derrida, *Apprendre à vivre enfin*. The title of this work is a reprise, and not by chance, of the famous phrase in *Spectres de Marx* with which Derrida eulogizes a philosophy of rebellion. Jacques Derrida died on 9 October 2004 from pancreatic cancer.

23. Dumas, *Le vicomte de Bragelonne*, 2:850.

SELECT BIBLIOGRAPHY

Afary, Janet, and Kevin B. Anderson. *Foucault and the Iranian Revolution*. Chicago: University of Chicago Press, 2005.

Allouch, Jean. *Louis Althusser: Récit divan*. Paris: EPEL, 1992.

Althusser, Louis. *Écrits philosophiques et politiques*. Vol. 1. Paris: Stock/IMEC, 1994.

———. *Écrits sur la psychanalyse*. Ed. Olivier Corpet and François Matheron. Paris: Stock/IMEC, 1993.

———. *Écrits sur la psychanalyse: Freud et Lacan*. Paris: Stock/IMEC, 1993.

———. "Freud et Lacan." In *Écrits sur la psychanalyse*, ed. Olivier Corpet and François Matheron. Paris: Stock/IMEC, 1993.

———. *Journal de captivité: Stalag XA, 1940–1945*. Paris: Stock/IMEC, 1992.

———. *L'avenir dure longtemps*, followed by *Les faits*. Ed. and with a preface by Oliver Corpet and Yann Moulier-Boutang. Paris: Stock/IMEC, 1992.

———. *Lettres à Franca 1961–1973*. Paris: Stock/IMEC, 1998.

———. *Pour Marx*. Paris: Maspero, 1965.

———. "Sur la révolution culturelle." *Cahiers Marxistes-Leninistes* 14 (November–December 1966).

Althusser, Louis, Étienne Balibar, Roger Establet, Pierre Macherey, and Jacques Rancière. *Lire "Le Capital."* Paris: Maspero, 1965.

Azouri, Chawki. *J'ai réussi là où le paranoïaque échoue.* Paris: Denoël, 1990.

Badiou, Alain. *Deleuze.* Paris: Hachette, 1997.

———. "Y a-t-il une théorie du sujet chez Georges Canguilhem?" In *Georges Canguilhem: Philosophe et historien des science,* 295–305.

Balibar, Étienne. *Écrits pour Althusser.* Paris: La Découverte, 1991.

Barthes, Roland. "De part et d'autre." In *Essais critiques.* Paris: Seuil, 1964.

Beauvoir, Simone de. *La force de l'âge.* 1960; Paris: Gallimard, 1991, in the series Folio.

Bénézech, Michel, and Patrick Lacoste. "L'uxoricide de Louis Althusser selon son récit autobiographique: Commentaires de psychiatrie criminelle." *Annales Médico-Psychologiques, Bulletin Officiel,* 1993.

Cabanis, José. *Les profondes années.* Paris: Gallimard, 1976.

Canguilhem, Georges. "Activité technique et création." In *Communications et discussions.* Société toulousaine de philosophie, 2e série, 1937–38, 81–86.

———. "Descartes et la technique." In *Travaux du XIe congrès international de philosophie.* Vol. 2. Paris: Hermann, 1937, 77–85.

———. *Études d'histoire et de philosophie des sciences.* Paris: Vrin, 1968.

———. *La Formation du concept de réflexe aux XVIIe et XVIIIe siècles.* Paris: PUF, 1955.

———. "La monstruosité et le monstrueux." In *La connaissance de la vie.* Paris: Vrin, 1965. Originally published 1962.

———. "Le cerveau et la pensée." In *Georges Canguilhem: Philosophe et historien des sciences,* 11–33.

———. *Le normal et le pathologique.* 1943; Paris: PUF, 1966.

———. "Mort de l'homme ou épuisement du cogito." *Critique* 242 (July 1967).

———. "Ouverture." In *Penser la folie: Essais sur Michel Foucault.*

———. Présentation of the colloquy "Michel Foucault, philosophe." Paris: Seuil, 1989.

———. "Qu'est-ce que la psychologie?" In *Études d'histoire et de philosophie des sciences.* Paris: Vrin, 1968. Originally published 1956.

———. "Sur l'*Histoire de la folie* en tant qu'événement." *Le Débat* 41 (September–November 1986).

———. "Une pédagogie de la guérison est-elle possible?" *Nouvelle Revue de Psychanalyse* 17 (Spring 1978): 13–26.

————. "Vie." In *Encylopedia universalis*, 1973. Vol. 16. ————. *Vie et mort de Jean Cavaillès*. Villefranche: Les Carnets de Baudasser, Pierre Laleur éditeur, 1976.

————. *A Vital Rationalist: Selected Writings from Georges Canguilhem*. Ed. François Delaporte, with an introduction by Paul Rabinow and a critical bibliography by Camille Limoges. Trans. Arthur Goldhammer. New York: Zone Books, 1994.

Castel, Robert. "Les aventures de la pratique." In *Le Débat* 41 (September–November 1986).

Char, René. *Feuillets d'hypnos*. Paris: Gallimard, 1946.

Chauvy, Gérard. *Aubrac: Lyon 43*. Paris: Albin Michel, 1997.

Contat, Michel, and Michel Rybalka. *Les écrits de Sartre*. Paris: Gallimard, 1970.

Deleuze, Gilles. *Deux régimes de fous: Textes et entretiens, 1976–1995*. Ed. David Lapoujade. Paris: Minuit, 2003.

————. *Différence et répétition*. Paris: PUF, 1969.

————. *Foucault*. Paris: Minuit, 1986.

————. *L'île déserte et autres textes: Textes et entretiens, 1953–1974*. Ed. David Lapoujade. Paris: Minuit, 2002

————. *Logique du sens*. Paris: Minuit, 1969.

————. *Pourparlers*. Paris: Minuit, 1990.

Deleuze, Gilles, and Félix Guattari. *Capitalisme et schizophrenie*. Vol. 1, *L'anti-Oedipe*. Paris: Minuit, 1972. Vol. 2, *Mille plateaux*. Paris: Minuit, 1980. Minuit published an augmented edition of *L'anti-Oedipe* in 1992 and republished both volumes of *Capitalisme et schizophrenie* in 2004.

Derrida, Jacques. *Apprendre à vivre enfin*. Interview with Jean Birnbaum. Paris: Galilée, 2005.

————. *Béliers: Le dialogue ininterrompu entre deux infinis, le poème*. Paris: Galilée, 2003.

————. *Chaque fois unique, la fin du monde*. Ed. Pascale-Anne Brault and Michael Naas. Paris: Galilée, 2003.

————. *L'écriture et la différence*. Paris: Seuil, 1964.

————. *Mémoires pour Paul de Man*. Paris: Galilée, 1988.

————. *Résistances de la psychanalyse*. Paris: Galilée, 1996.

————. *Spectres de Marx*. Paris: Galilée, 1993.

Derrida, Jacques, and Élisabeth Roudinesco. *De quoi demain . . . dialogue*. Paris: Galilée/Fayard, 2001.

Dosse, François. *Histoire du structuralisme.* Vol. 1, *1945–1966.* Paris: La Découverte, 1991.

Dreyfus, Hubert, and Paul Rabinow. *Michel Foucault, un parcours philosophique.* Paris: Gallimard, 1984.

Ellenberger, Henri F. *Histoire de la découverte de l'inconscient.* 1970; Paris: Fayard, 1994.

———. *Médicines de l'âme: Essais sur l'histoire de la folie et des guérisons psychiques.* Paris: Fayard, 1995.

Eribon, Didier. *De près ou de loin: Entretiens avec Claude Lévi-Strauss.* Paris: Odile Jacob, 1998.

———. *Michel Foucault et ses contemporaines.* Paris: Fayard, 1994.

———. *Michel Foucault.* Paris: Flammarion, 1991. In the collection Champs.

———. *Sur cet instant fragile: Carnets, janvier-août 2004.* Paris: Fayard, 2004.

Ferry, Luc, and Alain Renaut. *La pensée 68.* Paris: Gallimard, 1986.

Foucault, Michel. *Dits et écrits, 1954–1988.* 4 vols. Paris: Gallimard, 1994.

———. *Histoire de la folie à l'âge classique.* 1961; Paris: Gallimard, 1972.

———. *La volonté de savoir.* Paris: Gallimard, 1976.

———. *Les anormaux: Cours au collège de France, 1974–1975.* Paris: Gallimard/Seuil, 1999.

———. *Les mots et les choses.* Paris: Gallimard, 1966. English title, *The Order of Things.*

———. *Maladie mentale et psychologie.* Paris: PUF, 1954; 2nd ed., 1962.

———. *Moi, Pierre Rivière, ayant égorgé ma mère, ma soeur et mon frère: Un cas de parricide au XIXe siècle.* Présenté par Michel Foucault. Paris: Gallimard/Julliard, 1973. In the collection Archives.

———. *Naissance de la clinique.* 1963; Paris: PUF, 1972.

Freud, Sigmund. *The Complete Letters of Sigmund Freud to Wilhelm Fliess, 1887–1904.* Ed. and trans. Jeffrey Moussaieff Masson. Cambridge: Harvard University Press, 1985.

Furet, François. *Le passé d'une illusion: Essai sur l'idée communiste au XXe siècle.* Paris: Calmann-Lévy, 1995.

Gauchet, Marcel, and Gladys Swain. *La pratique de l'esprit humain: L'institution asiliare et la révolution démocratique.* Paris: Gallimard, 1980. English title, *Madness and Democracy: The Modern Psychiatric Universe.*

Georges Canguilhem: Philosophe et historien des sciences: Actes du colloque des 6–8 décembre 1990. Paris: Albin Michel, 1993, in the series Bibliothèque du collège international de philosophie.

Goldstein, Jan. *Console and Classify: The French Psychiatric Profession in the Nineteenth Century.* New York: Cambridge University Press, 1987. In French, *Consoler et classifier: L'essor de la psychiatrie française.* Paris: Les empêcheurs de penser en rond, 1997.

Goldstein, Kurt. *La structure de l'organisme.* 1934; Paris: Gallimard, 1983. In the collection Tel, with a preface by Pierre Fédida.

Granjon, Marie-Christine, ed. *Penser avec Michel Foucault: Théorie critique et pratiques politiques.* Paris: Karthala, 2005

Green, André. "Analyse d'une vie tourmentée." Interview with Catherine Clément. *Magazine Littéraire* 309 (November 1992).

Guattari, Felix. *Écrits pour L'anti-Oedipe.* Ed. Stéphane Nadaud. Paris: Lignes et Manifestes, 2005.

Guibert, Hervé. *À l'ami qui ne m'a pas sauvé la vie.* Paris: Gallimard, 1990.

———. "Les secrets d'un homme." In *Mauve le vierge.* Paris: Gallimard, 1988.

Hale, Nathan G., Jr. *Freud and the Americans.* 2 vols. New York: Oxford University Press, 1971–95. In French, *Freud et les Américains: L'implantation de la psychanalyse aux États-Unis.* Paris: Les empêcheurs de penser en rond, 2001.

Hirschmüller, Albrecht. *Josef Breuer.* 1978; Paris: PUF, 1991.

Huston, John. *An Open Book.* New York: Knopf, 1980. In French, *John Huston.* Paris: Pygmalion, 1982.

Jambet, Christian. "Y a-t-il une philosophie française?" *Annales de Philosophie* 10 (1989).

Jamet, Dominique. "Le crime du philosophe Althusser." *Le Quotidien de Paris,* 24 November 1980.

Lacan, Jacques. *De la psychose paranoïaque dans ses rapports avec la personnalité.* 1932; Paris: Seuil, 1975.

———. *Écrits.* Paris: Seuil, 1966.

———. "Le stade du miroir comme formateur de la fonction du je." In *Écrits,* 93–101. Originally published 1949.

———. "Le temps logique et l'assertion de certitude anticipée. Un nouveau sophisme." *Cahiers d'Art,* 1940–44. Republished in *Écrits* with numerous alterations.

Laing, R. D., and David Cooper. *Raison et violence.* Paris: Payot, 1963.

Lanzmann, Claude. *Shoah.* Paris: Fayard, 1985.

Lemoine-Luccioni, Eugénie. *L'Histoire à l'envers: Pour une politique de la psychanalyse.* Paris: Des femmes, 1992.

Macherey, Pierre. "Aux sources de l'*Histoire de la folie*: Une rectification et ses limites." *Critique* 471–72 (August–September 1986).

———. "De Canguilhem à Canguilhem en passant par Foucault." In *Georges Canguilhem: Philosophe et historien des science.*

———. "La philosophie de la science de Georges Canguilhem: Épistémologie et histoire des sciences." *La Pensée* 113 (1964): 50–74.

Major, René. *De l'éléction: Freud face aux idéologies américaine, allemande, et soviétique.* Paris: Aubier, 1986.

Marty, Éric. *Louis Althusser, un sujet sans procès: Anatomie d'un passé très récent.* Paris: Gallimard, 1999.

Masson, Jeffrey Moussaieff. *Le réel escamoté.* Paris: Aubier, 1984.

Michel Foucault, philosophe. Paris: Seuil, 1989.

Miller, James. *The Passion of Michel Foucault.* New York: Simon and Schuster, 1993. In French, *La passion Foucault.* Paris: Plon, 1995.

Moulier-Boutang, Yann. *Louis Althusser: Une biographie.* Paris: Grasset, 1992.

Penser la folie: Essais sur Michel Foucault. Paris: Galilée, 1992.

Péquignot, Henri. "Georges Canguilhem et la médicine." *Revue de Métaphysique et de Morale* 1 (January–March 1985): 39–51.

Piquemal, Jacques. "G. Canguilhem, professeur de terminale, 1937–1938." *Revue de Métaphysique et de Morale* 1 (January–March 1985): 63–83.

Pommier, Gérard. *Louis du néant: La mélancolie d'Althusser.* Paris: Aubier, 1998.

Postel, Jacques. *Genèse de la psychiatrie: Les premiers écrits de Philippe Pinel.* 1981; Paris: Les empêcheurs de penser en rond, 1998.

Revue de Métaphysique et de Morale. 1 (January–March 1985). A special issue dedicated to Georges Canguilhem.

Roudinesco, Élisabeth. *Histoire de la psychanalyse en France.* 1986; Paris: Fayard, 1994.

———. *Jacques Lacan: Esquisse d'une vie, histoire d'un système de pensée.* Paris: Fayard, 1993.

———. *La famille en désordre.* Paris: Fayard, 2002.

———. "La mémoire salie de Salvador Allende." *Libération*, 12 July 2005.

———. *Pourquoi la psychanalyse?* Paris: Fayard, 1999.

Roudinesco, Élisabeth, and Michel Plon. *Dictionnaire de la psychanalyse.* 1997; Paris: Fayard, 2006.

Saint-Sernin, Bertrand. "Georges Canguilhem à la Sorbonne." In *Revue de Métaphysique et de Morale* 1 (January–March 1985).

Sarraute, Claude. "Petite faim." *Le Monde*, 14 March 1985.

Sartre, Jean-Paul. "Autoportrait à soixante-dix ans." In *Situations X*. Paris: Gallimard, 1976.

————. *Carnets de la drôle de guerre, Novembre 1939–mars 1940*. Paris: Gallimard, 1983.

————. "Entretien sur l'anthropologie." *Cahiers de Philosophie* 2–3 (February 1966).

————. *La nausée*. Paris: Gallimard, 1938.

————. "La république du silence." In *Situations III*. Paris: Gallimard, 1949.

————. *Le mur*. Paris: Gallimard, 1939.

————. *L'engrenage*. In *La P. respectueuse*. Paris: Gallimard, 1954, in the series Livre de Poche. Originally published 1948.

————. *Le scénario Freud*. Preface by Jean-Bertrand Pontalis. Paris: Gallimard, 1984.

————. *Les mots*. Paris: Gallimard, 1964. In the collection Folio.

————. *Les mouches*. Paris: Gallimard, 1976. In the collection Folio.

————. *Les séquestrés d'Altona*. Paris: Gallimard, 1960.

————. *L'être et le néant*. Paris: Gallimard, 1943.

————. *Lettres au castor*. Vol. 1. Paris: Gallimard, 1988.

————. *L'existentialisme est un humanisme*. Paris: Nagel, 1946.

————. *L'idiot de la famille: Gustave Flaubert de 1821 à 1857*. 3 vols. 1971; Paris: Gallimard, 1988.

————. *Questions de méthode*. Vol. 1 in *Critique de la raison dialectique*. 1960; Paris: Gallimard, 1985. Originally published 1957.

Schneider, Michel. *Blessures de mémoire:* Paris: Gallimard, 1980.

Semelaigne, René. *Les pionniers de la psychiatrie avant et après Pinel*. 2 vols. Paris: Ballière et fils, 1930.

Sirinelli, Jean-François. *Génération intellectuelle: Khâgneux et normaliens dans l'entre-deux-guerres*. Paris: Fayard, 1988.

————. *Intellectuels et passions françaises: Manifestes et pétitions au XXe siècle*. Paris: Fayard, 1990.

Sollers, Philippe. *Femmes*. Paris: Gallimard, 1983.

Streicher, Frédéric. "À propos de *Différence et répétition*." *Sciences Humaines* 3 (May–June 2005).

Sulloway, Frank J. *Freud, Biologist of the Mind: Beyond the Psychoanalytic Legend*. New York: Basic Books, 1979. In French, *Freud, biologiste de l'esprit*. Preface by Michel Plon. 1981; Paris: Fayard, 1998.

Surya, Michel. *Georges Bataille: La mort à l'oeuvre*. Paris: Gallimard, 1992.

Swain, Gladys. "Chimie, cerveau, esprit: Paradoxes épistémologiques des psychotropes en médecine mentale." In *Dialogue avec l'insensé*. Paris: Gallimard, 1994, 263–79. Originally published 1987.

———. *Le sujet de la folie: Naissance de la psychiatrie*. 1977; Paris: Calmann-Levy, 1997.

Taguieff, Pierre-André. *Prêcheurs de haine*. Paris: Mille et une nuits, 2004.

Vernant, Jean-Pierre. *La traversée des frontières*. Paris: Seuil, 2004.

Winock, Michel. "Sartre s'est-il toujours trompé?" *L'Histoire* 296 (February 2005).